Essential Histories

The Napoleonic Wars (4)
The fall of the French empire 1813–1815

Essential Histories

The Napoleonic Wars (4)

The fall of the French empire 1813–1815

OSPREY
PUBLISHING

Gregory Fremont-Barnes

First published in Great Britain in 2002 by Osprey Publishing,
Elms Court, Chapel Way, Botley, Oxford OX2 9LP, UK
Email: info@ospreypublishing.com

© 2002 Osprey Publishing Limited

Every attempt has been made by the publisher to secure the
appropriate permissions for material reproduced in this book. If
there has been any oversight we will be happy to rectify the
situation and written submission should be made to the
Publishers.

ISBN 1 84176 431 0

Editor: Sally Rawlings
Design: Ken Vail Graphic Design, Cambridge, UK
Cartography by The Map Studio
Index by Bob Munro
Picture research by Image Select International
Origination by Grasmere Digital Imaging, Leeds, UK
Printed and bound in China by L. Rex Printing Company Ltd.

02 03 04 05 06   10 9 8 7 6 5 4 3 2 1

For a complete list of titles available from Osprey Publishing
please contact:

Osprey Direct UK, PO Box 140,
Wellingborough, Northants, NN8 2FA, UK.
Email: info@ospreydirect.co.uk

Osprey Direct USA, c/o MBI Publishing,
PO Box 1, 729 Prospect Ave,
Osceola, WI 54020, USA.
Email: info@ospreydirectusa.com

www.ospreypublishing.com

This book is one of four titles on the Napoleonic Wars in the
Osprey Essential Histories series

Contents

Introduction

By 1810 Napoleon had established an empire in Europe that surpassed that of Charlemagne a millennium before. Yet within the space of a few years it would collapse. This last volume in the series on the Napoleonic Wars will trace the events that led to its fall during the climactic years 1813–15, in which, among a host of other battles, were fought two of the most decisive

Napoleon and his forlorn staff lead the army through mud and snow during the campaign of 1814 in France. Despite the immense losses sustained by the *Grande Armée* the previous year, the Emperor steadfastly clung to his conviction that he could ultimately achieve victory, a belief underlined by his apparently callous indifference to losses. 'I grew up upon the field of battle,' Napoleon declared a few months before, 'and a man such as I cares little for the lives of a million men.' (Philip Haythornthwaite)

in history – Leipzig and Waterloo. Leipzig, the largest battle in history until 1914, became known as the 'Battle of the Nations' because of its sheer size and the number of nationalities involved. Half a million men struggled in a clash of arms that was to determine whether Napoleon would continue to maintain his empire in central Europe. What might, but for the extraordinary error on the part of a single sergeant of engineers, have been a drawn battle became a disaster that forced Napoleon and his shattered army to abandon Germany and retire across the Rhine, thereby bringing the war again to French soil for the first time in more than 20 years. The campaign of 1814 which followed taxed Napoleon to the limit, and yet, with paltry forces – some mere boys – he displayed some of his former strategic and tactical genius and inflicted a series of defeats on the Allies before succumbing to force of numbers and the betrayal of his marshals.

The seeds of destruction were sown during the Russian campaign in 1812, after which, despite having lost over half a million men, Napoleon prepared for a new campaign in the coming spring. The Russians, emboldened by Napoleon's retreat, were prepared to carry the war, which was to become the War of the Sixth Coalition, into Germany, with Prussia as a junior partner in a new alliance.

That this alliance had been preceded by five others provides a good indication of the Great Powers' failure to curb French expansion since the start of the wars two decades earlier. Yet for Prussia and for a number of other German states, this new struggle was to have an ideological component which had been absent from her war of 1806–1807: the campaign of 1813 was to become known by its patriotic title: the 'War of German Liberation'. The moral forces which had once given impetus to the armies of revolutionary France were now coming back to haunt them, though with some adaptations. The Prussians had no desire for a republic, but their nationalism had been

awakened, and the war was to be for the liberation of 'Germany', more than half a century before an actual nation state by that name emerged.

At this stage, the coalition did not contain all the Great Powers, yet unity was essential for success. Some nations, such as Austria and Sweden, wished to wait and see how the tide of fortune moved, but ultimately they and most of the former members of the Confederation of the Rhine, including Bavaria and Saxony, would side with the Allies in numbers which Napoleon could never hope to match. Britain, too, would play a vital diplomatic and financial role in the war, ensuring Allied unity and providing millions of pounds in subsidies to nations that could supply the manpower required. Britain had committed tens of thousands of men to the ongoing struggle in Spain, and continued to man the fleets which blockaded French ports and starved Napoleon's empire of seaborne trade.

Yet Napoleon was not to be daunted by circumstances that lesser commanders might have deemed hopeless. Quickly raising new armies composed of young, inexperienced conscripts and invalided veterans, but seriously deficient in competent non-commissioned officers (NCOs) and trained officers, and with a critical shortage of cavalry, Napoleon resolved to preserve his empire in Germany, despite the rapidly spawning forces of nationalism. The Emperor's organizational genius resurrected a new army with which he achieved hard-fought victories at Lützen and Bautzen before, in late summer, Austria finally threw in her lot with the Allies, thereby creating the most formidable military alliance Europe had ever seen and the combination of Great Powers that was absolutely essential if Europe was to free itself of Napoleon's control.

Further epic struggles were to follow in the autumn campaign, including the battles of Dresden and Leipzig. When operations shifted to French soil in 1814, the beleaguered Emperor found himself outnumbered by more than three to one, yet in a series of brilliant actions he managed to hold the Allies at bay, displaying a military genius reminiscent of his earlier years. Nevertheless, with Paris threatened, his army overwhelmed by vastly superior numbers, and his marshals refusing to fight on, Napoleon was ultimately forced to abdicate, only to return the following year to fight his last, and history's greatest, battle.

Waterloo was more than a battle with far-reaching political effects: it was a human drama perhaps unparalleled in military history, and it is no accident that far more has been written about this eight-hour period of time than any other in history. The defense of La Haye Sainte and Hougoumont, the charge of the Scots Greys, Wellington's steadfast infantry defying the onslaught of the cuirassiers, the struggle for Plancenoit, and the repulse of the Imperial Guard – all became distinct and compelling episodes in a battle on which hinged nothing less than the future of European security. When it was all over, the Allies could at last implement their extensive and historic plans for the reconstruction of Europe. Though these plans did not guarantee peace for the Continent, they offered a remarkable degree of stability for the next 40 years. Indeed, the Vienna Settlement, in marked contrast to those before it and since – especially that achieved at Versailles in 1919 – stands as the most effective and long-lasting political settlement up to 1945.

For both the ordinary ranks of Napoleon's army and for senior commanders, campaigning had always been accompanied by a degree of hardship, particularly after nearly 20 years of unremitting war. Yet the immediate wake of the Russian campaign was to render the campaigns of 1813 and 1814 especially hard, with march, countermarch, bivouac, hunger, thirst, rain, mud, cold, and privation. It would also be a time when commanders would be tested to the limit and the flaws in Napoleon's command structure would become glaringly apparent.

In the past, field commanders had seldom been allowed to coordinate their operations except with the express orders of Napoleon and little was done to encourage them to develop independent thought or initiative. Without adequate understanding of the Emperor's grand strategy or their own roles in it, Napoleon's subordinates could do little but follow orders unquestioningly at a time when armies had grown so much larger than in past campaigns that Napoleon simply could not oversee everything, and needed commanders capable of independent decision-making. By 1813 some of these had been killed in action (Desaix, Lannes, Lasalle), others would die in the coming campaign (Bessières and Poniatowski), and still more were simply tired of fighting or were busy in Spain. Some were excellent as leaders of men in combat, but were not themselves strategists and were reluctant to take independent decisions lest they fail.

With marshals constantly shifted from command of one corps to another and corps changing in composition as circumstances seemed to require, no viable command structure could be created. Proper control of increasingly poorer-quality soldiers became all the more difficult. Under such circumstances, with Napoleon unable to be everywhere and monitor everything, errors were inevitable, and at no time in his military career were these errors so glaring as in 1813–15.

FOLLOWING PAGE Despite the disaster in Russia, the empire remained impressive in size, consisting of an over-sized France that extended to the Rhine and across the Pyrenees, and including the Low Countries, parts of northern Italy and the Dalmatian coast. Direct Bonapartist rule extended to the Kingdoms of Italy (Napoleon himself), Naples (his brother-in-law Murat), Westphalia (his brother Jerome), and Spain (his brother Joseph). Switzerland and the Duchy of Warsaw were French satellites, together with the various states of the Confederation of the Rhine and France possessed other allies of varying loyalty, including Denmark–Norway, Prussia, and Austria, the last of which gave up its imperial princess, Marie-Louise, as Napoleon's bride in 1810. By the beginning of 1813 all this was under grave threat, with Russia, Britain, Spain, and Portugal hostile, and Prussia soon to join them.

Europe at the beginning of 1813

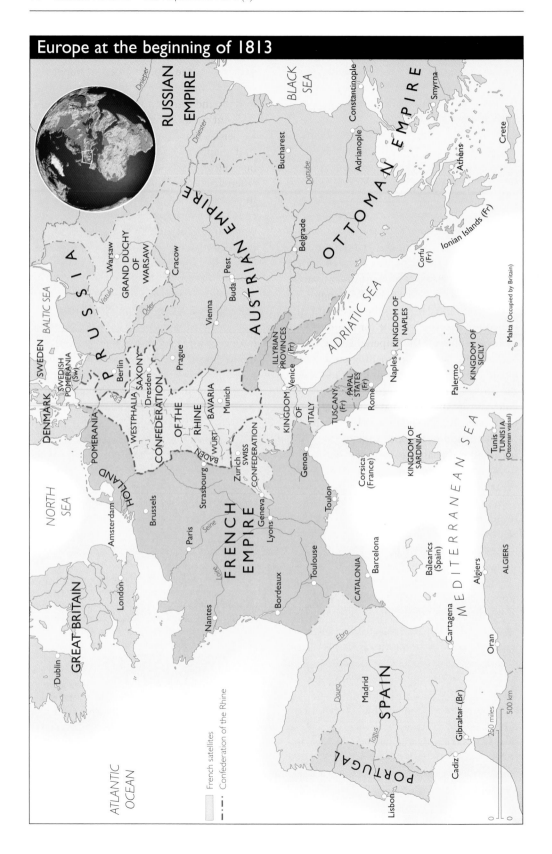

RUSSIAN EMPIRE

Dnieper

BLACK SEA

Smyrna

OTTOMAN EMPIRE

Constantinople

Adrianople

Athens

Crete

AUSTRIAN EMPIRE

Dniester

Bucharest

Danube

Belgrade

Ionian Islands (Fr)

Corfu (Fr)

Malta (Occupied by Britain)

Warsaw

GRAND DUCHY OF WARSAW

Cracow

Vistula

Oder

Buda

Pest

Vienna

Prague

ILLYRIAN PROVINCES (Fr)

Venice

ADRIATIC SEA

KINGDOM OF NAPLES

Naples

KINGDOM OF SICILY

Palermo

BALTIC SEA

SWEDEN

DENMARK

SWEDISH POMERANIA (Sw)

PRUSSIA

Berlin

POMERANIA

WESTPHALIA

SAXONY

Dresden

CONFEDERATION OF THE RHINE

BAVARIA

Munich

WÜRT

BADEN

KINGDOM OF ITALY

TUSCANY (Fr)

PAPAL STATES (Fr)

Rome

Genoa

Corsica (France)

KINGDOM OF SARDINIA

Tunis

TUNISIA (Ottoman vassal)

NORTH SEA

HOLLAND

Amsterdam

Brussels

Strasbourg

Zurich

SWISS CONFEDERATION

Geneva

Lyons

Toulon

MEDITERRANEAN SEA

GREAT BRITAIN

London

Dublin

FRENCH EMPIRE

Paris

Seine

Loire

Nantes

Bordeaux

Toulouse

CATALONIA

Barcelona

Balearics (Spain)

Algiers

ALGIERS

Ebro

SPAIN

Madrid

Cartagena

Oran

Douro

PORTUGAL

Tagus

Lisbon

Cadiz

Gibraltar (Br)

ATLANTIC OCEAN

French satellites
Confederation of the Rhine

250 miles

500 km

Chronology

1812   **5 December** Napoleon leaves the *Grande Armée* during the retreat from Moscow to return to Paris.

14 December Last elements of the *Grande Armée* cross the Niemen and enter Poland.

28 December General Yorck, commanding the Prussian corps in Russia, signs the Convention of Tauroggen, establishing the neutrality of his forces.

1813   **16 January** Russians resume their advance west, crossing the Vistula.

7 February Russian troops enter Warsaw unopposed. The French ally, the Duchy of Warsaw, ceases to exist.

28 February Prussia ratifies the preliminary agreement of Kalisch with Russia. King Frederick William and Tsar Alexander commit 80,000 and 150,000 troops, respectively, to the coming campaign.

3 March Britain and Sweden conclude the Treaty of Stockholm, by which, in exchange for subsidies, Sweden agrees to join the Sixth Coalition.

6 March French forces retreating eastwards reach the Elbe.

12 March French garrison evacuates Hamburg, one of the most important fortress towns east of the Rhine.

13 March Prussia declares war on France.

27 March Allied troops occupy Dresden, capital of Saxony.

3 April Battle of Möckern, the first serious engagement of the campaign; 30,000 French troops under Eugène surprise Wittgenstein's 50,000 Russo-Prussian Army, before withdrawing.

1 May French open their offensive in Germany. Fighting occurs at Poserna, as Ney and Marmont advance east in a general drive on Leipzig. Bessières is killed in action.

2 May Battle of Lützen. First major battle of the campaign. Both sides suffer 20,000 casualties, among them the Prussian chief of staff, Scharnhorst.

8 May French reoccupy Dresden.

20–21 May Battle of Bautzen. Second major confrontation of the campaign, between Wittgenstein and Napoleon, commanding 96,000 and 150,000 men, respectively. A French victory, but not wholly decisive, with both sides losing approximately 20,000 men.

28 May French forces under Davout reoccupy Hamburg and begin an active and largely successful campaign of minor actions against local Prussian forces.

1 June French troops reach Breslau, on the Oder.

4 June Napoleon and the Allies sign an armistice, effective until 20 July, but later extended to 16 August. Both sides use this breathing space to prepare for renewed hostilities.

7 July Sweden, under the former French marshal Bernadotte, joins the Allied coalition.

19 July Austria concludes the Convention of Reichenbach. Emperor Francis promises to join the Allies if Napoleon refuses peace terms designed to be unacceptable.

12 August Austria declares war on France after Napoleon rejects terms which would eliminate French influence east of the Rhine.

13 August Prussian troops advance, terminating the armistice three days early.

23 August Battle of Grossbeeren. First of several Allied victories achieved over Napoleon's subordinates. French lose 3,000 to the Allies' 1,000.

26 August Action at Pirna. Minor action in which 32,000 French under Vandamme defeat 12,500 under Prince Eugène near Dresden.

26–27 August Battle of Dresden. Major French victory between approximately 150,000 Allies and 70,000 French. Allied casualties: 38,000; French: 10,000.

30 August Battle of Kulm. Vandamme, with 32,000 men, is isolated and badly defeated, losing half his men and falling captive. Allied morale partly restored and effect of Dresden partly mitigated.

6 September Battle of Dennewitz. Prusso–Swedish force of 80,000 under Bernadotte confront Ney with 55,000, near Berlin. French defeat costs 10,000 men to the Allies' 7,000.

24 September French troops withdraw behind the Elbe.

6 October Treaty of Ried. Austria recognizes Bavaria as an independent kingdom in exchange for her defection to the Allies.

9 October Battle of Düben. Blücher withdraws before Napoleon's arrival threatens serious defeat.

14 October Battle of Liebertwolkwitz. Major cavalry action between Murat and Wittgenstein, preliminary to the general confrontation between the main armies at Leipzig.

16–18 October Battle of Leipzig. Culminating and decisive engagement of the campaign in Germany, involving nearly 500,000 combatants over three days. Allies lose 55,000 to French 68,000. Napoleon retreats to the Rhine, abandoning military and political control over Germany.

18 October Württemberg and Saxony join the Allies, their troops defecting in the course of the fighting at Leipzig.

30 October Battle of Hanau. Bavarians under Wrede, irresponsibly deployed and seriously outnumbered, foolishly attempt to block French retreat to the Rhine and are badly mauled by Napoleon.

22 December Elements of the Allied forces begin crossing the Rhine into France.

1814   11 January King Murat of Naples joins the Allies.

14 January Denmark concludes peace with the Allies at Kiel.

22 January Prussian forces cross the river Meuse in France.

27 January Battle of St Dizier. Blücher, with 25,000 Prussians, defeats Victor and advances on Brienne before Napoleon, in close pursuit, can reach the scene of action.

29 January Battle of Brienne. Napoleon, with 30,000 raw recruits, inflicts 4,000 casualties on Blücher for 3,000 of his own, but is nevertheless unable to prevent the Allied push against Paris.

1 February Battle of La Rothière. Blücher, with 53,000 men, supported by 63,000 other troops in the area, forces battle on Napoleon, with under 40,000. Effectively a drawn action, both sides lose about 6,000 men.

3 February Negotiations for peace begin at Châtillon-sur-Seine.

10 February Battle of Champaubert; start of the Six Days' Campaign. Napoleon strikes Blücher's isolated army on the Marne, destroying part of it for a negligible loss to himself.

11 February Battle of Montmirail. Napoleon routs a Russian corps under Sacken, causing temporary consternation to the Allies and obliging Blücher to withdraw toward Rheims.

12 February Battle of Château-Thierry. Pursuing retreating elements of Blücher's command, Napoleon catches Yorck's rearguard, inflicting 2,700 casualties for a loss of only 600 of his own.

14 February Battle of Vauchamps. Napoleon's fourth victory against the Allies in the course of the month. Blücher withdraws, with 7,000 killed and wounded to the French 600.

17 February Battle of Valjouan. Marching his Imperial Guard 46 miles (75 km) in 36 hours, and employing the entire Paris garrison, Napoleon attacks Wrede's corps of 60,000 men, driving it off.

18 February Battle of Montereau. Pursuing Schwarzenberg's retreating forces, Napoleon assaults positions prepared by the Allies, forcing their retreat and inflicting 6,000 casualties to 2,500 of his own.

21 February Napoleon proposes a new peace plan to Francis; this is rejected.

25 February Allies establish a war council at Bar-sur-Aube and outline a new strategy in light of recent failures.

27–28 February Action at Meaux. Driving on Paris, Blücher repeatedly fails to dislodge Marmont, and redirects his march north of the Marne.

7 March Battle of Craonne. Blücher's numerically superior army fights an inconclusive action with Napoleon east of Paris. Both sides lose about 5,000 men.

9 March Treaty of Chaumont. The Allies finally agree on campaign objectives: Napoleon is offered peace terms based on the French frontiers of 1791; in the event of rejection, the Allies agree not to conclude a separate peace until final victory; Britain offers massive subsidies to support the campaign.

9–10 March Battle of Laon. The most significant action of the campaign, Napoleon's forces narrowly escape destruction as military and political collapse grows imminent.

13 March Battle of Rheims. Napoleon surprises a Russian corps, driving the defenders from the city and causing 6,000 casualties for a trifling loss to himself.

20 March Battle of Arcis-sur-Aube. Ambushed and nearly routed, Napoleon's army rallies to hold off determined attacks, but the arrival of large numbers of Allied reinforcements forces a French withdrawal.

24 March Allies hold war council at Sommagices. Learning from captured documents that the defenses of Paris are incomplete, the inhabitants panicking and opposition to Napoleon rampant, the Allies march both their main armies directly against the capital.

25 March Battle of La-Fère-Champenoise. Last major action of the campaign. 20,000 Allies practically annihilate 4,000 conscripts under Mortier and Marmont, while 20,000 surviving French troops make haste toward Paris.

31 March French troops at Montmartre and in Paris surrender. While Napoleon himself is far to the east, nearly 150,000 Allied troops move against the capital, where Mortier and Marmont put up a brief but spirited resistance with 25,000 forlorn troops, before further resistance appears futile.

6 April Napoleon abdicates unconditionally after the Allies reject his offer of a regency for his son.

16 April Treaty of Fontainebleau gives Napoleon sovereignty over Elba. He departs for the island on 28 April.

17 April Marshal Soult surrenders to Wellington in southern France, ending the Peninsular War.

30 April Treaty of Paris concluded between the victorious Allies and the restored Bourbon monarch, Louis XVIII, bringing a formal end to the war. France to retain frontiers of 1792, including large parts of the Rhineland; French West Indian colonies ceded to Britain; further territorial and political questions to be discussed at Vienna later in the year.

1 November Proceedings of the Congress of Vienna begin, dominated by Russia, Britain, Austria, and Prussia. Restoration, territorial compensation, and international security form the central features of discussion.

1815 **1 March** Napoleon escapes from Elba and lands in France.

14 March Ney, sent by the king to intercept him, defects, together with his troops, to Napoleon at Auxerre.

15 March King Murat of Naples, pledging support for his former emperor, declares war on Austria.

20 March Napoleon enters Paris; beginning of the 'Hundred Days'.

25 March Allied representatives, still conferring at Vienna, agree to form a Seventh Coalition.

2–3 May Neapolitans defeated by the Austrians at Tolentino; Murat flees his kingdom on 19 May but is caught and executed.

9 June Congress of Vienna terminates business just as Napoleon's return renews the threat to general European security.

15 June Napoleon, hoping to defeat the Anglo–Dutch and Prussian armies before the other Allies can advance from the distant east, crosses the river Sambre into Belgium.

16 June Battle of Quatre Bras. Ney launches determined attacks against Wellington, but as Anglo–Dutch reinforcements appear throughout the day the action is drawn.

16 June Battle of Ligny. Fought simultaneously with Quatre Bras. Napoleon confronts the Prussians under Blücher, each side numbering approximately 80,000. After bitter attacks and counterattacks the Prussian center ultimately collapses, but darkness renders French victory incomplete and Blücher withdraws intact.

18 June Battles of Waterloo and Wavre. While Grouchy engages the Prussian rearguard at Wavre, 9 miles (15 km) west of Waterloo, Napoleon and Wellington, the latter providentially reinforced later in the day by Blücher, fight the final, decisive battle of the Napoleonic Wars.

22 June Napoleon abdicates. Later he surrenders to British authorities, who refuse his request for sanctuary in England.

8 August Napoleon departs England aboard HMS *Northumberland*, bound for exile on the extrmely remote south Atlantic island of St Helena, where he dies in 1821.

26 September Holy Alliance concluded at Vienna. A vague international agreement inspired by Alexander, principally intended for Austria, Russia, and Prussia, that binds their sovereigns to govern on Christian principles.

20 November Second Treaty of Paris. France is reduced to her 1790 frontiers, heavy indemnities imposed and Allied occupation troops are to remain until payment is fulfilled.

Origins of Prussian and Russian hostility

Germany in ferment, 1807–1812

Prussia's involvement in the campaigns of 1813–15 may be traced back to the autumn of 1806, when, having remained aloof from the Third Coalition, she foolishly confronted Napoleon with only Saxony at her side and with the Russian armies too far to the east to be of assistance before winter. Prussia had smarted at Napoleon's creation of the Confederation of the Rhine in the heart of Germany, and the French refusal to cede Hanover (formerly a British possession) as promised, convinced King Frederick William III (1770–1840) that the time had come to put into the field his armies, widely acknowledged to be the best in Europe. The twin decisive victories at Jena and Auerstädt on 14 October destroyed the illusion of Prussia's superiority and in a matter of weeks practically the whole of her forces were rounded up or besieged in fortresses and obliged to capitulate.

Seeing the vaunted Prussian ranks broken at Jena and Auerstädt was shocking enough for contemporaries, but to witness the systematic hunting down of the remnants of the army and the pitifully feeble resistance offered by fortresses throughout the kingdom in the weeks that followed was more than the nation could bear. Years of French occupation were to follow. The Treaty of Tilsit, concluded

Meeting at Tilsit, July 1807. While France and Russia settled their differences and established an alliance which recognized Napoleonic mastery of western and central Europe, Prussia was left truncated and humiliated: a new French satellite, the Kingdom of Westphalia, absorbed all Prussian territory west of the Elbe; Prussia was stripped of her Polish possessions to create another satellite, the Grand Duchy of Warsaw; Danzig was created a free city; Prussia was forced to join the Continental System; and, finally, French troops were to remain on her soil until enormous war indemnities were paid in full. (Ann Ronan Picture Library)

in July 1807, imposed subordination and in its wake Napoleon took deliberate and concerted measures to reduce not only Prussia's pride and prestige, but her military and economic power. Her status as a great power was effectively lost as Napoleon raised the status of smaller German states like Saxony, to which he allotted all Prussian territory in her former Polish province, while imposing a series of harsh restrictions on Prussia, including a massive indemnity of several hundred million francs. The much revered Queen Louise (1776–1810), symbol of Prussia's former grandeur and pride, had to endure numerous personal insults under French occupation, including Napoleon's description of her as 'the only real man in Prussia', and the queen's subjects attributed her premature death to such indignities. French troops occupied Prussia's fortresses on the Oder and her ports on the Baltic, while the Continental System destroyed the kingdom's seaborne commerce. Large parts of her territory were ceded to the French puppet state of Westphalia and her army was restricted to 42,000 men for 10 years. By all these measures and others, Prussia was left severely – but not fatally – weakened, and with her pride badly wounded she would remain a potentially dangerous time-bomb in the years after Tilsit.

The result was a movement of reform and growing patriotism, some of it exposed for all to see, though much of it kept secret so as to avoid French detection and suppression. Young Prussians established the anti-French *Tugendbunde* ('League of Virtue'), and other societies which encouraged not simply a narrow form of Prussian patriotism, but a kind of pan-German unity that demanded freedom from foreign domination in general, but French in particular. At official levels reforms were undertaken by men like Baron Stein (1757–1831), who worked in a civilian capacity, and by Gerhard von Scharnhorst (1755–1813) and Augustus von Gneisenau (1760–1831), who introduced new and sometimes radical changes within the army. Though aware of many of these activities, Napoleon did not fear Prussian attempts at

Queen Louise of Prussia. Revered by her subjects as the soul of national virtue, Louise openly advocated war with France in 1806 and regularly referred to Napoleon as 'the Monster'. On taking up the challenge, the Emperor announced in his *Bulletin* to the army, 'A beautiful queen wants to see a battle. So, let us be gallant and march at once …' The two did not come face to face until the historic meeting at Tilsit in July 1807, by which time Prussia had been comprehensively beaten and occupied. (Ann Ronan Picture Library)

social, economic and military reform, for he believed Frederick William to be too timid to challenge French might. In any event, his kingdom had neither the financial nor the military resources to wage a war of national resistance.

For five years the Prussians suffered under Napoleonic occupation, their passionate hatred of the French and desire for vengeance growing more intense as the years passed. Such sentiments, whether overtly anti-French or simply pro-German, had been fostered and promoted by the philosophies of Immanuel Kant (1724–1804) and Johann Fichte (1762–1814). Before long, Prussians began to channel their discontent into thoughts of patriotism, embracing notions hitherto

Augustus Wilhelm, Count von Gneisenau. A general in the Prussian Army, Gneisenau worked with Scharnhorst in implementing wide-ranging military reforms between 1807 and 1813, including new principles for officer training, the establishment of a general staff, and the introduction of a system of reservists, by which large numbers of men could be trained, released back into civilian life and then called up on short notice to swell the ranks of the army. He performed well as Blücher's Chief of Staff from 1813 to 1815. (Philip Haythornthwaite)

It is only by means of the common characteristic of being German that we can avert the downfall of our nation, which is threatened by its fusion with foreign peoples, and win back again an individuality that is self-supporting and quite incapable of any dependence on others … we alone must help ourselves if help is to come to us … By means of the new [system of] education we want to mould the Germans into a corporate body … The German, if only he makes use of all his advantages, can always be superior to the foreigner … he alone is capable of real and rational love for his nation.

These ideas had an impact on civilians, both among young intellectuals and the nation as a whole, and also profoundly affected the officer corps, including men like Karl von Clausewitz (1780–1831), who would later attain even greater prominence with his magnum opus, *Vom Kriege* ('On War'). Not only did Prussian soldiers adopt the battle cry 'Das Vaterland!' in place of 'Der König!', but they were retrained to employ entirely new methods and tactics introduced by specially convened commissions that scrapped the obsolete system employed by the armies of Frederick the Great (1713–86). These were replaced with drills, organization, tactics, and technology, based on careful studies of Napoleonic innovation. The reformers abolished corporal punishment, much like in the French Revolution, as unworthy of men fighting for the 'nation' or 'fatherland', so that a soldier might follow his officers out of respect rather than fear. Just as in French revolutionary reforms, merit overcame aristocratic privilege as the principal criterion by which eager young men committed to national service acquired a commission and subsequent promotion.

The Prussian Army had been strictly limited to 42,000 men by Napoleonic *dictat*. Prussian military reformers now adopted an ingenious method of circumventing this restriction, enabling them to train more soldiers without exceeding the official size of the army. A system of shrinkage (*Krümpersystem*) was introduced by which men called to the colors received intensive

connected with the French Revolution, particularly the concepts of 'nation' and, in a peculiarly German form, 'fatherland'. Unlike the French, however, the Prussians did not regard such revolutionary principles as entirely incompatible with monarchy.

Wholesale military reforms were introduced in tandem with social reforms, which in turn fostered a growing sense of German nationalism between 1807 and 1813. In his *Addresses to the German Nation*, delivered in the winter of 1807–08 but which provided a model for many others to follow, Fichte defied the French occupiers with a less than subtle appeal for resistance to Napoleonic rule:

training, and joined the ranks for a limited time before being released back to civilian life. These recruits would later be recalled for further periods of training to maintain a reasonable level of fitness and acquaintance with military life, but once demobilized they became a sort of hidden reserve, which by the beginning of 1813 amounted to 80,000 men – in addition to the standing army. Therefore, as the spring campaign season opened, Prussia was reasonably ready – with Russia taking a leading role – to challenge Napoleonic authority, for spiritual and military preparations had been under way for five years. It was clear, moreover, that the winter retreat had inflicted a devastating blow to French arms, and the sight of the shattered remains of the *Grande Armée* shuffling on to Prussian territory emboldened those who were already inclined to resist the occupation.

Resistance emerged elsewhere in Germany during this period. When Austria again opposed France in 1809, Napoleon subdued her yet again, taking Vienna in May, suffering a temporary check at Aspern–Essling, and finally emerging victorious at Wagram on 5 July. By the Treaty of Schönbrunn (14 October), Emperor Francis I (1768–1835) ceded land to the Confederation of the Rhine, to Saxony, and to the Kingdom of Italy. Russia, by then in possession of Swedish Finland, received part of Austria's Polish territories in Galicia. Francis, playing for time in which to recover and reorganize both his army and his shattered finances, offered Napoleon – now divorced from the Empress Josephine (1763–1814) – the hand in marriage of his daughter, the Archduchess Marie-Louise (1791–1847), and the two produced a son, Napoleon II (1811–32), born on 20 April 1811, and known as the 'King of Rome'.

Hereafter, signs of growing German resistance became particularly marked. Not only had Austria risen up, but many individual Germans began to question the legitimacy of French domination of central European affairs. Already in 1806 the French had executed a bookseller from Nuremberg

Emperor Francis I of Austria. Under Francis Austria was a consistent opponent of both Revolutionary and Napoleonic France, fielding armies in numerous unsuccessful campaigns (1792–97, 1800, 1805, 1809) which reduced the vast Habsburg territories in Italy, Poland, and along the Adriatic coastline. After first seeking to appease Napoleon by offering his daughter, Marie-Louise, in marriage, Francis ultimately threw in his lot with the Allies in August 1813, and accompanied his army until the fall of Paris. (Philip Haythornthwaite)

named Johann Palm (1768–1806) for printing and distributing anti-French literature. In 1809 a young Thuringian, bent on assassinating Napoleon and in so doing accelerating the French withdrawal from Germany, was executed. And in the following year Andreas Hofer (1767–1810), who had raised the standard of revolt in the Tyrol just prior to the campaign of 1809, was also executed. The French had also demanded that the Prussian government arrest and hand over their foreign minister, Stein, for alleged conspiracies against France, and only Stein's refuge in Russia prevented a lengthy prison term and possibly death. Such heavy-handed policies against German patriots, accused of treason while merely questioning the French presence in their midst, began to effect a profound change in German attitudes.

Franco–Russian relations, 1805–1812

Russia had been instrumental in forming the Third Coalition in 1805 (including Austria, Britain, Sweden, and Naples) and had contributed substantial military resources to the campaign that ended disastrously for the forces of Tsar Alexander I (1777–1825) and his Austrian allies at Austerlitz, in Moravia, on 2 December of that year. Austria soon abandoned the coalition, while Alexander withdrew his army through Bohemia – his men badly shaken but not crushed.

When Prussia challenged France in the autumn of 1806, Russia prepared to assist her, but military intervention did not become effective until early 1807, by which time Prussia had been thoroughly beaten, and the costly struggle at Eylau on 7 February and, finally, the decisive defeat at Friedland on 14 June, persuaded Alexander to seek terms with Napoleon, in conjunction with the Prussian king. The peace of Tilsit the following month sparked a diplomatic revolution, converting France and Russia from adversaries into allies, with Europe split between them and a chastened Frederick William in control of a much weakened Prussia. By secret clauses in the treaty France promised to assist Russia in 'liberating' most of European Turkey, while in return Russia agreed to open hostilities with Britain and Turkey if Britain refused the Tsar's mediation.

Both sides promised to pressure Sweden, Denmark and Portugal into conforming to the Continental System – Napoleon's ambitious scheme to close the whole European coastline to British commerce in an attempt to strangle the British economy. Russia cooperated, albeit unenthusiastically, and duly declared war on Britain in November (and invaded Swedish territory in 1808), though war with Britain amounted to

Alexander I of Russia. The Tsar's formidable forces opposed the French in 1805 and 1807, before Napoleon finally decided to invade Alexander's vast empire. Despite the occupation of Moscow, Alexander not only refused to negotiate, but pursued the French out of Russia and across Germany in a relentless campaign to reach Paris and overthrow the Bonaparte dynasty. Russia's major contribution to victory and Alexander's considerable influence on affairs at the Congress of Vienna established Russia as the most powerful nation on the Continent until the Crimean War. (Philip Haythornthwaite)

little more than the cessation of trade with her. Napoleon and Alexander renewed their agreement at a conference at Erfurt in September 1808, while French armies were busy in Spain trying to subdue that nation as part of the same scheme to eradicate British trade with the Continent.

That close Franco–Russian relations never fully developed may be divined by Alexander's decision to stand aloof during the 1809 campaign, his armies merely observing on the Austrian frontiers. With victory achieved over Austria for the fourth time since 1792 (1797, 1800 and 1805), Napoleon's new friendship, such as it was, with the Habsburg monarchy caused considerable concern at St Petersburg, and in any event by 1810 Russia was growing tired of the economic hardship caused by her inability to carry on trade with Britain. Pro-British factions in the court of St Petersburg were now once again in the ascendant and there were signs that Napoleon was not fulfilling his side of the Tilsit agreement. He had raised the Electorate of Saxony to the status of a kingdom and had created the Kingdom of Westphalia for his brother Jerome out of Prussian territory, but the Emperor had done nothing to hasten the partition of Turkey, and Russia continued to wage her war against the Ottomans, begun in 1806, without any French aid. Moreover, the territory of the Duke of Oldenburg, a relation of Alexander's, was annexed to France without prior consultation. Russian anxieties grew still deeper when, in 1810, Napoleon not only annexed Holland in order better to enforce the Continental System, but also extended his control along the coastline stretching to the Baltic Sea. Both these actions were clear violations of Tilsit.

For his part, Alexander had also broken his commitments. He faithfully closed his ports to British merchant vessels, yet British and colonial goods still came ashore via ships flying neutral flags and protected by Royal Navy escorts. The fact remained that, by 1810, the exclusion of British commerce had badly injured the Russian economy; by employing this expedient, Alexander could improve his financial situation by collecting import duties on such goods. By the end of the year he had also increased the duty on French imports coming by land – yet another source of grievance. The Tsar also grew increasingly resentful of the French satellite, the Grand Duchy of Warsaw – a Polish state reconstituted from Prussian and Austrian annexations of the partitions of the 1790s – and suspected the French of involvement in the Swedes' nomination of the former Napoleonic marshal, Jean-Baptiste Bernadotte (1763–1844), to their throne, as crown prince. Thus, through a combination of many factors based on mutual mistrust and self-interest, the

Franco–Russian alliance established in 1807 had effectively ceased to exist by 1811.

By this time Napoleon, grown tired of Russian refusals to support the ban on British trade, planned his ill-fated invasion, and on 24 February 1812 he enlisted Prussia's nominal support in the form of 20,000 men, augmented by 60,000 Austrians supplied in conformity with a treaty concluded on 12 March. Together with his own *Grande Armée* of genuinely loyal troops – half of whom hailed from outside France herself – the Emperor had 600,000 men ready by the spring. Alexander, for his part, was not idle. Apart from assembling large forces of his own, on 5 April he established an offensive and defensive alliance with Sweden – finding Bernadotte in fact hostile to Napoleon – and on 28 May he ended his six-year war with Turkey, thus releasing much needed troops for the theater of war to the north.

At the end of March, through secret overtures to Frederick William, he learned that Prussia's support for the invasion was nothing more than a demonstration, with an auxiliary corps of 20,000 men under Major-General Yorck von Wartenburg (1759–1830), while the Austrians indicated on 25 April that their army, under Prince von Schwarzenberg (1771–1820), would not take part in serious fighting. In July Britain and Russia happily signed a treaty of peace, ending the quasi-war that Tilsit had created. For the first time since April 1805, during the formation of the Third Coalition, these two peripheral, yet powerful, nations entered into a formal alliance by which Britain promised subsidiary aid and weapons, while Russia prepared to oppose the French invasion with her enormous resources in manpower.

Napoleon's invasion began on 22 June, he fought a costly struggle at Borodino on 7 September and entered Moscow the same month. Weeks passed as he waited for the Tsar to come to terms. Receiving no communication and with most of the city already destroyed by fire, Napoleon began the long winter retreat, with its now well-known and fatal consequences. (See Essential Histories *The Napoleonic Wars (2) The empires fight back*).

Opposing forces

The *Grande Armée*

The catastrophic losses suffered in the Russian campaign had so profound and multi-faceted an effect on the *Grande Armée* as to require virtually its complete reconstitution for the start of the campaign of 1813. Of the approximately 655,000 troops with which Napoleon had crossed the Niemen in June 1812, scarcely 100,000 bedraggled, broken men staggered into East Prussia little more than six months later. Of the 1,300 pieces of field artillery that had accompanied the army into Russia, only about 250 guns remained, most of the others having been simply abandoned due to lack of transport.

Notwithstanding these unprecedented losses, Napoleon immediately set to work to revive his shattered army, demonstrating in the process the organizational genius that had contributed so much to the construction of that institution which had made the empire possible in the first place. Napoleon must be given credit for the almost miraculous effort through which he recreated the *Grande Armée* out of the wreckage of 1812. His vision was ambitious indeed: 656,000 men, and he set about drawing together troops from various sources which ultimately netted him about 400,000, of whom half constituted the field army when hostilities opened in April. A high proportion of the new levies were very young and came to be called the 'Marie-Louises', after the Empress who in 1812 ordered their assembly on behalf of the absent Emperor. With admirable foresight Napoleon had called up the class of 1813 before the Russian campaign. These consisted of about 130,000 conscripts in the process of completing training, 80,000 National Guardsmen placed in the ranks of the regulars, and 100,000 more men who had, for various reasons, not joined the colors between 1809

and 1812. To all these were added troops withdrawn from Spain, from which they could not be spared without adverse effects on that theater of operations. Finally, patient British blockading had trapped naval vessels in ports for years, rendering their crews useless. These underemployed men and others from the coastal garrisons, particularly marines, were sent east where they could be of more immediate use.

As far as equipment and matériel were concerned, feverish efforts were under way on the home front, as the Marquis de Caulaincourt (1773–1827) observed:

France is one vast workshop. The entire French nation overlooked his reverses and vied with one another in displaying zeal and devotion … It was a personal triumph for the Emperor, who with amazing energy directed all the resources of which his genius was capable into organizing the great national endeavour. Things seemed to come into existence as if by magic …

France, with a population of over 30 million, was certainly productive, but one essential commodity could not be manufactured: horses. Shortage of horses was one of the most serious deficiencies suffered by Napoleon's forces at the opening of the spring campaign of 1813. While the ranks of the infantry could, as a result of exceptional efforts, be filled with the young and the old, and while guns could be found in depots or manufactured anew, the complete replacement of lost horseflesh proved impossible.

In all the various arms that required horses in Russia – the artillery, the sundry transport services, and of course the cavalry itself – losses numbered between 160,000 and 200,000. These were not merely woeful, but irreparable losses, depriving Napoleon of the mounted patrols required for proper reconnaissance, in addition to cavalry for ordinary combat and pursuit operations. After the Russian campaign new mounts would never remotely match Napoleon's stated requirements, nor could the numbers or quality of the troopers themselves be replaced, for even where a horse could be provided, it required three times longer to train a cavalryman than a simple foot soldier, and such training could not be provided on the march. Thus, deficiencies in cavalry simply could not be made good in the time available. The same, of course, applied to the artillery, a specialized arm that required time to acquaint officers and their crews with the science of gunnery. Here, too, the guns required horses to pull them, as did the thousands of supply wagons that accompanied the army. An obvious expedient lay in stripping formations posted elsewhere in the empire, and therefore Napoleon issued immediate orders for the transfer of most of his cavalry from Spain. This, however, would take time.

Yet time, like men and horses, was in short supply. The Russians were approaching from the east and the Prussians had yet to commit themselves. There is no doubt that French soldiers would often fight bravely in the campaigns ahead, but their efforts were frequently hamstrung by inadequate training and experience at all levels, and this resulted in a decline in their fighting capabilities. Colonel Raymond de Montesquiou, Duc de Fezensac, attributed the French defeats of 1813 to the decline in the quality of the soldiers.

The Army was composed of young soldiers who had to be taught everything, and of non-commissioned officers who did not know much more themselves. The officers were better, for they were old cadres who had suffered far less destruction in Russia than had the N.C.O. cadres.

But the process had begun even before 1812. As early as 1809, he noted, Napoleon began to complain that his soldiers were not like those of 1805: the men at Wagram were not like those at Austerlitz. By 1813, the new army was not even up to the standards of Wagram. 'No doubt,' de Fezensac continued:

there were moments of élan, and fine examples of gallantry. When the generals marched in the front rank, the troops were inspired by their example, but this enthusiasm was short-lived, and the heroes of one day displayed nothing but despondency and weakness on the morrow. It is not on battlefields that soldiers go through the severest ordeals: French youth has an instinct for bravery. But a soldier must be able to put up with hunger, fatigue, bad weather; he must march day and night in worn-out shoes, must brave the cold and the rain with his uniform in tatters, and do all this without grumbling and while staying in a good humour. We have known men like this; but it was asking too much of young fellows whose constitution was barely formed and who, to start with, could not have the military spirit, the 'religion' of the colours, and that moral energy which doubles a man's strength while doubling his courage.

Nevertheless, no other nation in Europe and no political leader could have accomplished so much with the resources and time available. Napoleon's achievement must be seen in this light.

As for the French allies, they remained loyal at least in name – Denmark, the Confederation of the Rhine, the Italian states – but many of these, particularly the Germans, were disaffected by the experiences of the Russian campaign, where they were often treated as second-class troops, and during the autumn campaign they largely defected, aligning themselves with the Allies. The Polish contingent from the Duchy of Warsaw was effectively destroyed in the previous campaign, and the Russian advance in February 1813 prevented all but a token reconstitution of an armed force.

The Russian Army

The Tsar's forces were impressive both in numbers and doggedness. Major-General Sir

Robert Wilson (1777–1849), British military commissioner attached to Alexander's headquarters, found Russian troops:

... endowed with great bodily strength ... with martial countenance and complexion; inured to the extremes of weather and hardship; to the worst and scantiest food; to marches for days and nights, of four hours' repose and six hours' progress; accustomed to laborious toils, and the carriage of heavy burdens; ferocious, but disciplined; obstinately brave, and susceptible to enthusiastic excitements; devoted to their sovereign, their chief, and their country. Religious without being weakened by superstition; patient, docile, and obedient; possessing all the energetic characteristics of a barbaric people, with the advantages engrafted of civilisation ...

If such a force appeared unstoppable, it must be observed that the campaign of 1812 had cost the Russian Army a great many experienced officers and men – an estimated 250,000 casualties. Friedrich von Schubert, of German parentage but a senior quartermaster on the Russian General Staff, commented

that by 1812 its quality had markedly declined, largely from losses and from the creation of new, less experienced regiments.

The constant wars had taken away many of the old soldiers, and the young ones did not have the same traditions; nor could they feel the same attachment to their corps as the old ones did.

John Spencer Stanhope, a British civilian traveling with the Russian Army in Germany, considered them impressive soldiers:

I found them a fine and hardy race, almost insensible to pain: they were, indeed, men of

Cossacks. Irregular horsemen with exceptional riding abilities and endurance but lacking discipline. Cossacks generally shied away from direct contact with cohesive units on the battlefield, concentrating instead on harrying their opponents' flanks and rear, raiding, reconnaissance and skirmishing. Cossacks were notorious looters and their presence in Germany was dreaded as much by the local populace as by the French themselves. On the fall of Paris in 1814 the Cossacks established their camp in the Bois de Boulogne, attracting many a curious spectator. (Peter Hofschröer)

iron. I remember seeing one coolly smoking his pipe, whilst the surgeon was cutting and slashing at him, in order to extricate a [musket] ball; and though I witnessed the sufferings of many of their wounded men, I do not think that I heard a single one utter a groan. They really seemed to be made of different stuff from other men: their frames and sinews were, apparently, as hard as their minds …

Observers seem to agree that the junior officers were appalling, perhaps because, with no opportunity for advancement, there was little incentive to display leadership.

The Cossacks were the most curious element of the army – wild, irregular, extremely adept horsemen from the steppes of the Don and Dniester who specialized in raiding and reconnaissance rather than the massed charges of their regular counterparts in the cavalry. Wilson described them thus:

Mounted on a very little, ill-conditioned, but well-bred horse, which can walk at the rate of five miles an hour with ease, or, in his speed, dispute the race with the swiftest – with a short whip on his wrist (as he wears no spur) – armed with the lance, a pistol in his girdle, and a sword, he never fears a competitor in single combat … They act in dispersion, and when they do re-unite to charge, it is not with a systematic formation, but en masse, or what in Germany is called the swarm attack … Dexterous in the management of a horse that is guided only by the snaffle, they can twist and bend their course through the most intricate country at full speed.

The Austrian Army

Like Prussia, Austria had acted as a nominal, but reluctant ally of France during the invasion of Russia, but its army had seen virtually no action and, though it did not participate in the spring campaign, Napoleon had no illusions that Francis was still a friend. When the armistice ended Austria boasted the largest army in Europe, with 429,000 men in uniform, of whom

Prince Schwarzenberg. A veteran of Austria's campaigns against the Turks and the French Revolutionaries, Schwarzenberg managed to avoid falling into French hands when General Mack surrendered his army at Ulm in 1805. In 1812 he led the Austrian corps that reluctantly accompanied the *Grande Armée* into Russia, but deliberately avoided confrontation with the Tsar's forces. When Austria joined the Sixth Coalition in August 1813, Schwarzenberg was appointed C-in-C of the Allied armies and led them to victory during the Leipzig campaign and the invasion of France. (Philip Haythornthwaite)

approximately 300,000 were available for actual operations in the Army of Bohemia, and by the end of the year the army's ranks would swell to over half a million. During the summer British subsidies helped alleviate the deficiencies in equipment and money needed to prepare Habsburg forces for the coming campaign. There were of course veterans of the 1809 campaign in its ranks, but the army had gleaned no combat experience in Russia and over 60 percent of the troops were inexperienced, obliged to complete their training on campaign. Overall, the army was of good quality, and when Sir Charles Stewart watched a review near Prague in mid-August he was suitably impressed, even if such troops would have been specially well-drilled for the occasion:

The composition of this army was magnificent, although I perceived a great many recruits: still the system that reigned throughout, and the military air that marked the soldier...must ever fix it in my recollection as the finest army of the continent ....[T]heir movement was beautifully correct, and the troops seemed formed in the most perfect order.

The cavalry he thought particularly impressive and the artillery, though perhaps not as well-equipped as the Russians', was nevertheless staffed by '...officers and men [who are] scientific and expert, and the artillery is not to be judged of by its appearance.'

The Prussian Army

Prussia and her army had learned many lessons since the catastrophic events of 1806–07. The defeats at Jena and Auerstädt were catalysts for fundamental reforms, beginning with the appointment of Graf Lottum and General Scharnhorst to lead the newly created Military Reorganization Commission. In 1807 this body recommended that the nobility lose its monopoly on officer commissions, that universal military service be adopted, and that hitherto draconian methods of military discipline be relaxed. Their recommendations soon bore fruit: by the end of 1808 new regulations put a stop to advancement based solely on seniority, and permitted any man with the requisite educational qualifications to hold a commission in any branch of the army. Corporal punishment was abolished, a new system of organization was adopted for the army as a whole, and the old style of strict linear tactics was replaced with new formations much more in keeping with the effective advances so palpably demonstrated by the French.

Thus, by the time Prussia was ready to fight France again, in 1813, men such as Scharnhorst, Clausewitz and Yorck had made great strides in modernizing the Prussian

Recruitment office for Lützow's *Freikorps* in Breslau, Silesia. In March 1813, Major Adolf Lützow (1782–1834) officially sponsored the formation of a free corps of patriotic Germans eager to liberate German soil. Independent units such as these were employed away from the main battlefields to harass French communications, rear formations, and to foment insurrection in towns occupied by Napoleon's troops. Improvements in discipline, equipment, and combat experience enabled Lützow's unit to become amalgamated into the regular Prussian forces in 1814. (Philip Haythornthwaite)

Army, including the introduction of new tactics for all arms that shook off much of the army's outdated 18th-century practices. Such men introduced new, more democratic regulations on the selection of officers, with regulations issued by the king in 1808 establishing the principle that:

... a claim to officer rank shall in peacetime be warranted only by knowledge and education, in time of war by exceptional bravery and quickness of perception. From the whole nation, therefore, all individuals who possess these qualities can lay title to the highest positions of

honour in the army. All social preference which has hitherto existed ceases completely in the army, and everyone, without regard to his social background, has equal duties and equal rights.

The Prussian Army regulars and militia took on thousands of volunteers in this climate of enthusiasm, and many units were so overwhelmed by young boys wishing to serve as drummers and buglers that many of them had to be rejected. Supply of proper

Crown Prince Bernadotte of Sweden. Commander of the Army of the North, he had previously served Napoleon as a Marshal, particularly distinguishing himself in the Austerlitz and Jena campaigns, before falling foul of the Emperor after Wagram. When elected Crown Prince of Sweden the following year his ties with Napoleon were severed forever. Bernadotte's disinclination to commit his troops against his own countrymen was caustically remarked upon by many at Allied headquarters. (Philip Haythornthwaite)

soldiers, however, could not keep pace with the army's unceasing demands, and resort was made to a comprehensive system of compulsory enlistment.

Conscription provided Prussia with an army very different from that inherited from Frederick the Great which had fought in the campaigns of 1806–1807. Many units in 1813 represented a true cross-section of society, as a battalion commander recorded of his men in the East Prussian *Landwehr* (national militia):

Beside a grey-haired man you might find a boy of seventeen; beside a worthy family-man, who had never conceived the idea of taking up arms while in the quiet circle of his civil profession, might be a gay adventurer; beside an educated young man, who had broken away from the happiest circumstances so as to fight for the Fatherland with high ideas of duty and honour, stood a raw youth.

In terms of size, again the reforms had achieved a great deal, for although the Treaty of Tilsit had strictly limited the army to 42,000 men, this had been cunningly circumvented so as to enable Prussia, by the opening of the campaign season of 1813, to supply 80,000 men. Nevertheless, after years of occupation by French and French-allied troops, Prussia had few funds with which to clothe, equip, and arm her men, and great reliance was placed on shipments of these commodities from Britain, who supplied muskets and uniforms in large quantities. Moreover, while the king issued a decree embodying 110,000 men of the *Landwehr*, enthusiasm for the war could not entirely compensate for fighting efficiency impaired by lack of training and a critical shortage of equipment – and many units resorted to using axes, farm tools, pikes, and obsolete firearms.

Sweden

Sweden provided troops during the autumn campaign of 1813 as part of the Army of the North, which also contained Russian and Prussian contingents. By the time of the

Leipzig campaign the Swedes numbered nearly 65,000 men, the infantry of average quality, their artillery of iron rather than brass, their equipment inferior to their contemporaries, and their cavalry indifferently mounted. Their chief deficiency lay at the most senior level, for their commander-in-chief, Bernadotte, though a former Marshal of the French Empire with considerable battlefield experience, was reluctant to commit his troops to battle. His was a delicate balancing act, for he did not wish to upset his countrymen with the horror of heavy casualties, nor did he particularly wish to inflict them on the soldiers of his native home, which it was often supposed he wished to rule once Napoleon was defeated and deposed.

Britain

Britain, with a population of only 12 million, maintained a small army committed to the ongoing campaign in Spain, where her forces occupied the attention of over 200,000 French troops. Her other major commitment was the Royal Navy's comprehensive blockade of French ports. As in all previous campaigns against Revolutionary and Napoleonic France,

The retreat from Moscow. Setting out in winter conditions, the much-reduced *Grande Armée* not only faced Cossacks and partisans harrying its flanks and rear, but an over-stretched and vulnerable supply system that completely collapsed as temperatures plummeted and snowfall increased. Russian regular forces also pursued, nearly trapping Napoleon's main body at the crossing of the Beresina in late November. Marshal Ney (center) heroically led the rearguard and is reputed to have been the last man to leave Russia. (Philip Haythornthwaite)

Britain would supply massive amounts of arms, ordnance and supplies to the Allies, together with unprecedented subsidies exceeding £26 million for the period 1813–15. From the beginning of the autumn campaign the amount of matériel and other items shipped for the use of the Russian, Prussian, Austrian, and Swedish armies was impressive, including over 200 cannon, complete with transport and ammunition, over 120,000 firearms, over 18 million rounds of ammunition and 23,000 barrels of powder, over 30,000 swords and sabers, 150,000 complete uniforms and 187,000 yards of cloth, over 1.5 million pounds of beef, biscuit, and flour, over 175,000 boots and shoes, 28,000 gallons of brandy and rum, and tens of thousands of other items such as knapsacks, clothing, saddles, and canteens.

A bid for revenge

Although the origins of the War of the Sixth Coalition may be found in the treaty of alliance established between Britain and Russia in June 1812, it was not clear until after the retreat from Moscow that this cooperation between such far-flung allies would develop into a coalition embracing Prussia, and Austrian intentions were far from clear. The immediate origins of the war, therefore, may be found in the snows of Russia, where the catastrophic retreat of the *Grande Armée* – ordered without due regard for historical precedent and against the advice of sounder heads – laid the basis for wider European resistance. Pursued by the Russian Army, local partisans and, of course, the ubiquitous Cossacks, Napoleon's seemingly endless columns withered away under fatigue, hunger, exposure, and constant harassment, culminating in the horrific crossing of the Beresina river at the end of November. Already a shadow of its former self, the army of frost-bitten and starving souls suffered further losses when over 25,000 soldiers and camp-followers were caught on the wrong side of the river, with the bridge unable to bear the traffic. The émigré Comte de Rochechouart related the horrific scene in his memoirs:

Nothing in the world more saddening, more distressing! One saw heaped bodies of men, women and even children; soldiers of all arms, all nations, choked by the fugitives or hit by Russian grapeshot; horses, carriages, guns, ammunition waggons, abandoned carts. One cannot imagine a more terrifying sight than the appearance of the two broken bridges, and the river frozen right to the bottom … Peasants and Cossacks prowled around these piles of dead, removing whatever was most valuable … On the bridge I saw an unfortunate woman sitting; her legs dangled outside the bridge and were caught in the ice. For twenty-four hours she had been clasping a frozen

child to her breast. She begged me to save the child, unaware that she was holding out a corpse to me! She herself was unable to die, despite her sufferings, but a Cossack did her this service by firing a pistol in her ear so as to put an end to her appalling agony.

On 5 December Napoleon mounted a sledge, abandoned what remained of his shattered army and made haste for Paris, there to raise a new army against a vengeful Russia and an almost inevitably resurgent Prussia, which by this stage was Napoleon's unwilling ally.

Back in France, circumstances were also looking grim. General Claude de Malet (1754–1812) had attempted a coup, and the disaster in Russia had been of such a magnitude that even Napoleon's hitherto masterful propaganda could not conceal the fact. In the famous 29th Bulletin, dated 17 December 1812, he reported to his incredulous people the destruction of the *Grande Armée*. The writing was on the wall and the news created shock and disbelief in some and outright terror in the minds of others. Just before midnight on 18 December the cannon at the *Invalides* boomed out, announcing the return of the Emperor to Paris. But the news of the disaster in Russia had preceded him, and Colonel de Fezensac, an aide de camp to Marshal Berthier (1753–1815), on leave in Paris, observed that time was running out:

The Emperor was invincible no longer. While we were dying in Russia, another army was perishing in Spain, and in Paris an obscure conspirator had tried to seize power. The campaign of 1813 was about to open, but in what circumstances! The defection of Prussia was no longer in doubt; the Austrian alliance was at the least very shaky; and the exhaustion of France increased in proportion as the list of her enemies grew longer. The stories told by officers who had survived the retreat contributed to intensify people's fear. Paris, used as she had been to songs of victory during the previous fifteen years, was learning day by day and with pained surprise the details of some fresh public or private calamity … people were shocked to see the Emperor entertaining at the Tuileries. It was an insult to public grief and revealed a cruel insensitivity to the victims. I shall always remember one of those dismal balls, at which I felt as if I were dancing on graves.

The shock was particularly great, not simply because of the scale of the catastrophe, which was revealed by news sent home by the survivors, but because France had long since come to expect victory followed by victory. The Emperor's valet, Wairy Constant (1778–1845), recalled the mortification pervading society, for it was 'the first time that Paris saw him come back from a campaign without bringing with him a fresh peace which the glory of his arms had won.' A deep sense of foreboding pervaded the country, the feeling that, as Talleyrand put it: 'the beginning of the end, and … the end itself could not be far distant.' As a first step to consolidate his support in the empire, Napoleon sought peace with the Pope through a new concordat. Meanwhile, far to the east, the Russians continued their march west, approaching Prussian soil and the Duchy of Warsaw, which they would soon occupy. The French evacuated the Polish capital between 4 and 8 February.

As discussed earlier, during the Russian campaign Prussia had furnished an auxiliary corps under Yorck, subordinate to Marshal Macdonald. But on 30 December Yorck concluded a secret convention with the Russian General Diebitsch at Tauroggen, which then converted Prussian troops under his command from French allies to neutrals, with an implicit part of the agreement being that they would soon join the Russians. Frederick William initially repudiated the agreement, anxious not to confront Napoleon anew, however weakened the Emperor now appeared to be. Yet the king could not hold back the rising tide of nationalism within his country, led predominantly by young Prussians –

Generals Diebitsch and Yorck meet on Christmas Day, 1812. While the French northern flank was busy retreating from Riga, Russian troops under Diebitsch managed to isolate Yorck's contingent of 17,000 disaffected Prussians. Five days of negotiations resulted in the Convention of Tauroggen, by which Yorck rendered his corps neutral, so establishing the precedent for Prussia's *volte face* and active participation against the French occupier. (Philip Haythornthwaite)

though other Germans as well. Hawkish elements within court circles, together with many senior officers, such as Generals Yorck, Blücher, and Bülow, exerted still further pressure on the otherwise feeble-minded and dithering monarch.

With the nation seething with revolt, on 28 February Prussia secretly concluded with Russia the Convention of Kalisch, committing Prussia to join the war in the coming weeks, in return for Russian recognition of Prussia's pre-1806 frontiers. The king was heavily influenced by Baron Stein, the exiled Prussian minister, who had become one of the Tsar's advisers. He frankly told the king, who had maintained a sort of paternalistic relationship with Alexander for over 10 years, not to prevaricate, for the populace of East Prussia, not to mention Yorck's troops, were already in revolt against Napoleon, and that retention of the throne required him to satisfy his own people's expectations and join forces with Alexander. Notwithstanding Frederick William's

continued hesitation and fear of the consequences, Prussia formally declared war on France on 13 March, unleashing feelings of pent-up hatred against her neighbor which were to manifest themselves in future conflicts stretching well into the twentieth century. If the king harbored doubts, the nation did not. The sentiments of one battalion commander summed up the mood when he wrote of this period in his memoirs:

This was a splendid time of noble enthusiasm … In the conviction that individuals as well as whole nations could achieve their destiny by great effort and noble deeds alone, everybody was resolved to do every manly action, [and] was ready for any sacrifice, in order to help liberate the Fatherland.

Austria, for her part, declared her neutrality and quietly withdrew her

ABOVE Staggering out of Russia in January 1813, the remnants of the *Grande Armée* reached safety either in East Prussia (as shown here) or the Duchy of Warsaw. On the 7th, a British liaison officer with the Russian Army reported that 16,000 bodies were left behind in Vilna, only 50 miles (80 km) from the Polish frontier, rendering the streets '… almost impassable, so filled they were with the dead bodies of men, and horses, and broken carriages &c.' (Peter Hofschröer)

RIGHT With the destruction of the *Grande Armée* in Russia, operations shifted to Germany, where by the spring of 1813 Napoleon had raised a new army to oppose the Russians and Prussians. Despite numerous disadvantages Napoleon initially performed fairly well, with victories at Lützen (2 May) and Bautzen (20–21 May), and the capture of Dresden (7–8 May). Nevertheless, after Austria joined the coalition in August, Allied fortunes improved, with a series of reverses inflicted on Napoleon's subordinates at Grossbeeren (23 August), the Katzbach (26 August), Kulm (29–30 August), and Dennewitz (6 September). Napoleon did manage to secure an important victory at Dresden (26–27 August), but his comprehensive defeat at Leipzig (16–18 October) forced him to retreat back to France, drubbing the Bavarians at Hanau (30 October) en route.

Theater of operations in Germany, 1813

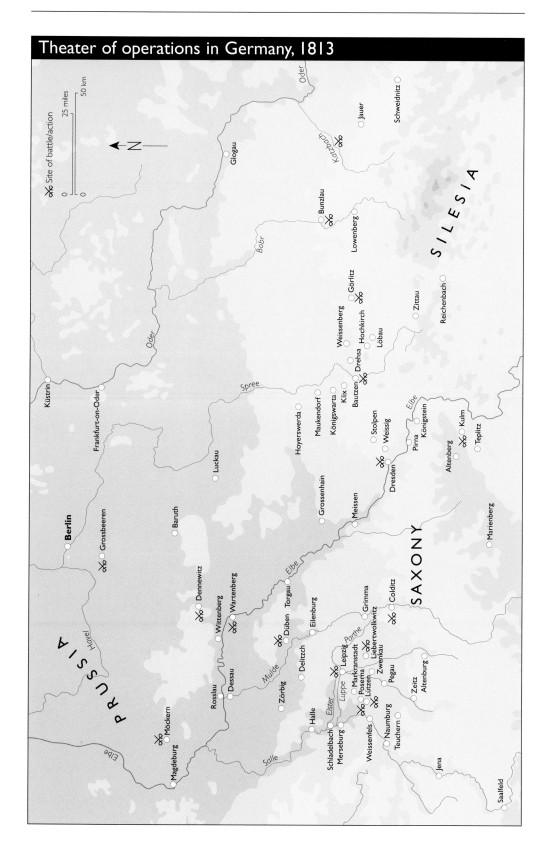

Frederick William III, King of Prussia. Indecisive and undistinguished, he doomed his country to eventual disaster by declining to join Austria, Russia, and Britain in the War of the Third Coalition in 1805. When he finally confronted France in 1806 he did so before the Russian armies could participate in the opening campaign. Even in the wake of the disastrous retreat from Moscow, Frederick William hesitated to throw in his lot with Russia until domestic political pressure and increasingly strident calls from the army obliged him to join the Sixth Coalition in 1813. (Ann Ronan Picture Library)

contingent, marching it to Bohemia via Warsaw, and thus providing a wide avenue through which the Russians could advance if, as it appeared, they wished to carry the war into the Napoleonic empire itself.

By the Convention of Kalisch, Russia had promised to deploy at least 150,000 men, but had only mustered about 120,000 by April. These were to be led by the veteran of the 1812 campaign, Field Marshal Michael Kutusov (1745–1813), who, in common with most of the other senior generals, was not enthusiastic about pursuing the French and risking the army in Germany. Russian troops had already suffered quite appallingly in the winter campaign of 1812 – almost as badly as the French – and were now operating along lines of communications extending hundreds of miles. Kutusov and other generals were on the whole satisfied with having seen them off Russian soil. Not so the crusading Tsar, who wished to avenge the destruction of Moscow by taking Paris, and to be seen as the liberator of Germany. Kutusov, Alexander insisted, was to assume the offensive and cross the Elbe.

The 'War of German Liberation' and the invasion of France

In grand strategic terms Napoleon understood the seriousness of his predicament at the beginning of 1813, but by no means despaired of his prospects. Austria remained neutral; Prussia, though hostile, could be overthrown again and her capital occupied; Russia, finding herself isolated, would be defeated in turn. The Tsar's army had, for the most part, not offered battle during the advance on Moscow; now that they were looking for a fight, they would have it – and suffer the long-sought blow which had eluded Napoleon at Borodino. Britain, though enjoying increasing success in Spain and continuing her strangling blockade of the European coastline, could be dealt with once the remainder of continental resistance had been subdued and the threat to the empire eliminated.

When the remnant of the *Grande Armée* emerged from Russia in December 1812 it established itself in Poland and East Prussia, under the temporary command of Marshal Joachim Murat (1767–1815). Before departing for Paris Napoleon had issued hopelessly unrealistic orders that Murat, with fewer than 40,000 men, should defend the line of the Vistula. French garrisons remained scattered in the fortresses of Danzig, Stettin, and Glogau-on-the-Oder, but there was little to stop the Russian advance. Kutusov did in fact halt behind that river in order himself to recover from the extreme rigors of the campaign, and to await supplies and reinforcements. But he did not remain stationary for long, and on 16 January 1813 he resumed his march west, occupying Warsaw unopposed on 7 February. Murat withdrew further, toward Posen, leaving 30,000 troops under General Jean Rapp (1772–1821) to hold the port of Danzig, and smaller contingents to occupy Thorn and Modlin. But Murat wanted nothing more to

do with operations, and after command devolved on Eugène de Beauharnais (1781–1824), Napoleon's step-son (the former Empress Josephine's son), Murat returned to Naples, of which he had been king since 1808.

Eugène appreciated that it was hopeless to defend Posen: his troops were exhausted, camped amidst a population seething with revolt, and faced by Russian forces whose advance across the frozen rivers could not be stopped. Fortunately for him, he was not expected to, as new orders arrived, calling on him to hold the River Oder. He therefore withdrew westward to Frankfurt, where he linked forces with a corps under Marshal Gouvion St Cyr (1764–1830). Combined French forces now totaled 30,000, but news that the Russians had already passed the Oder to the north obliged the French to retire west yet again, first in the direction of Berlin and then to Wittenberg, a city on the Elbe. The French arrived on 6 March, but soon discovered that the river was too long to defend. All in all, the Emperor's expectations were too grand, and six days later the French evacuated Hamburg. Eugène was only being realistic, appreciating as he did – and Napoleon did not – that the quality of his men left much to be desired and that popular dissent was growing throughout Germany.

With the assurance of direct Russian assistance as laid down by the Convention of Kalisch the previous month, Frederick William declared war on France on 13 March, and by the end of the month Napoleon, still in Paris, was aware of the fact. Prussia's defection posed an immediate, though not necessarily fatal, danger to the French position in Germany. From Marienwerder, General Wittgenstein (1769–1843) was moving west, soon joined by Generals Yorck and Bülow, with whose forces Wittgenstein now had 40,000 men. Kutusov, with about 30,000 men, stood near Kalisch, while the Russian advance guard under General Winzingerode (1770–1818), numbering 13,000, was considerably forward into Saxony, where it joined forces with 25,000 Prussians under General Gebhard von Blücher (1742–1819). This combined force then moved on Dresden, which it occupied on 27 March. At the same time Bernadotte had mustered a force of 28,000 men in Pomerania, while 9,000 Anglo–Hanoverians were in the vicinity of Stralsund.

The first major action of the campaign occurred at Möckern, where on 3 April Eugène attacked Wittgenstein, whose defeat nevertheless did not prevent the Russian commander from linking up with Blücher, then at Dresden. With Allied efforts at concentration now well under way, Eugène decided to abandon the upper Elbe and withdrew to the river Saale, whose strength would provide Napoleon with the precious time he required to raise sufficient numbers of troops to oppose the Allies with some prospect of success.

Ever since he had returned to Paris in December, Napoleon had been busily employed in trying to raise new armies. Various expedients were resorted to: extending conscription, transferring troops from Spain, and heavy drafts of National Guardsmen into the regular army. Recourse to these drastic measures paid considerable dividends – at least in numerical terms – yielding about 200,000 men by early April, while the Ministry of War continued its efforts of furnishing at least part of the Emperor's further requirements of another 450,000 troops. Napoleon began to deploy approximately 120,000 men at the River Main, consisting of four corps plus the Imperial Guard. Elsewhere, Eugène had 58,000 men at the Saale, Marshal Louis-Nicolas Davout (1770–1823) led 20,000 west of Hamburg and 14,000 cavalry under Horace Sébastiani (1772–1851) were stationed along the lower Elbe. The army was grievously deficient in cavalry, but it

nevertheless outnumbered the Allies in the vicinity, who totaled about 110,000 men.

The spring campaign

Napoleon's forces nevertheless fell short of the 300,000 he believed he required, a shortfall partly attributable to the absence of contingents expected from Bavaria and Saxony, which had not yet raised new forces to replace those lost in Russia. In spite of these problems Napoleon decided on an offensive in the direction of Berlin and the besieged cities of Danzig, Thorn, and Modlin. At the same time the Allies began their own offensive from Dresden toward the Saale. Napoleon's plans were therefore temporarily postponed.

Fairly confident that Napoleon was planning to attack the Allies, Blücher and Wittgenstein, exercising caution, had been moving west across and beyond the Elbe, and by 9 April their patrols had reached the area around Saalfeld. Though themselves outnumbered, they placed their confidence in their superior mobility, and planned to attack part of Napoleon's forces before his corps could be concentrated. By the middle of April this strategy, accepted by Alexander and Frederick William, was well under way, and with them on their march to the front were reinforcements which, by 24 April,

1. Lauriston attacks Kleist's bridgehead at Lindenau, crosses the Elster and takes the village. Kleist retreats.
2. 11.30 pm Full-scale Allied attack against Ney. Blücher advances toward Kaja and Grossgörschen. Allies open cannonade with 45 guns. French withdraw first behind Grossgörschen and then Kaja.
3. 1.00 pm–6.30 pm Napoleon orders Ney to hold Kaja and adjacent villages. Support from Macdonald and Latour-Maubourg on his left and Bertrand and Marmont on his right intended to trap Allies in double envelopment. Bitter fighting leaves Ney barely in possession of Kaja, but Allies hold Grossgörschen, Kleingörscher and Rahna. Many villages change hands several times in the course of the day.
4. 6.00 pm Wittgenstein launches his last reserves. Fierce fighting between Russians and Macdonald's division. By 9.00 pm Eugène as far as Eisdorf.
5. 6.30 pm–7.00 pm Young Guard retakes Kaja, but Grossgörschen remains in Prussian hands. Allies abandon field around 10.00pm.

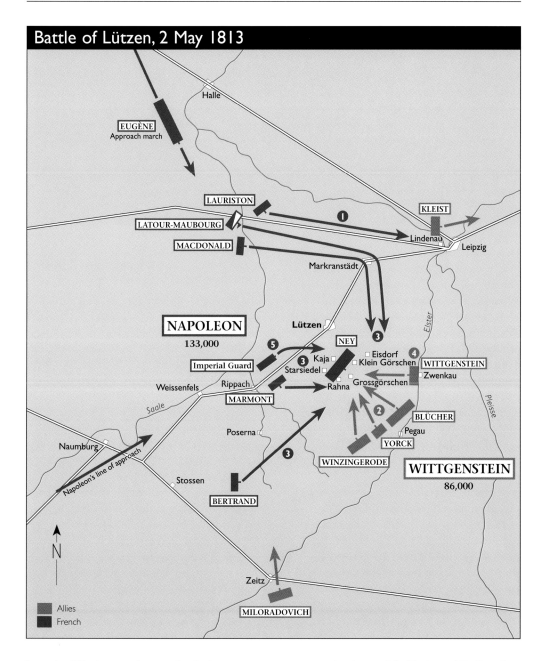

Battle of Lützen, 2 May 1813

brought Allied strength near the Saale to 73,000, including 25,000 cavalry and over 500 guns.

Starved of the cavalry requisite for reconnaissance duties, Napoleon developed a two-pronged strategy: to oppose the Russian advance by moving his main army as far as the Saale, with Eugène's army on its left; and to launch a counteroffensive in the direction of Dresden in order to cut Prussian

communications with Silesia and Berlin. On 1 May the French armies began their march toward Leipzig by proceeding east over the Saale.

As Eugène made for Schladelbach, Napoleon pushed two columns – one under General Bertrand (1773–1844) and Marshal Oudinot (1767–1847), the other led by Marshals Ney (1769–1815) and Marmont (1774–1852) – toward Naumberg and Lützen.

Meanwhile the Allied commanders were caught up in a dispute over the successor to Kutusov, who had fallen ill from exhaustion in late April and died a few weeks later. News of the French advance obliged them to settle their differences quickly, and command devolved on Wittgenstein, a fairly junior yet competent general officer who ordered forces to concentrate for a thrust against the French right flank near Lützen. The first day's fighting centered around Poserna, where the Allies launched furious attacks, while the second day's fighting focused on Lützen itself, where Ney's corps was hit by strong forces under Wittgenstein. The French emerged victorious but, without adequate cavalry, they could not exploit their success.

Nevertheless, Lützen restored the army's confidence in its chief and reminded the Allies, who retreated east, that Napoleon would not easily be beaten. Not satisfied with an incomplete victory, Napoleon divided his main body in two on 4 May, moving the larger contingent toward Dresden, where intelligence reported the presence of some of Wittgenstein's force, and ordering the remaining troops under Ney to proceed north-east where they were to defend the Elbe crossings at Wittenberg and Torgau. He was also to incorporate the Saxon Army into his forces as soon as the king gave his consent.

At Allied headquarters, meanwhile, new disputes arose – this time on Prussian fears for the safety of their capital, fears exacerbated by Ney's advance. Senior commanders reached a compromise: an

Prussian infantry advancing up the Kreckwitz Heights at Bautzen. Following the Allied defeat at Lützen earlier in the month, Wittgenstein assumed a new defensive position around Bautzen, 31 miles (50 km) east of the Elbe, deploying 96,000 men against Napoleon's 150,000. The Prussians played a significant part in the fighting alongside their Russian allies and were particularly hard-pressed in the second day's combat when Soult's 20,000 infantry attacked Blücher's fortified positions, seizing the fort at Kreckwitz before stalling due to inadequate artillery support. (Peter Hofschröer)

unengaged corps under General Friedrich von Bülow (1755–1816) would defend Berlin while the Prussian main body would retire beyond the Elbe to confront the French at Bautzen. Eugène challenged the Prussians at Colditz on 5 May, and the Prussians' failure to destroy the bridges at Dresden behind them three days later enabled Napoleon to establish his men in the suburbs on the same day and to make defensive bridgeheads on the opposite bank of the Elbe on 9 May.

Having established that the Allies were concentrating around Bautzen, Napoleon did the same, recalling Ney's corps from the north and attacking over the course of 20 and 21 May. Again a decisive victory had eluded him because of a shortage of cavalry for pursuit operations and as a result of Ney's having neglected to sever the Allies' lines of retreat. New arguments arose among the Allies as a consequence of their defeat, resulting in Barclay de Tolly (1761–1818) replacing Wittgenstein as commander of Russian forces and the decision to effect a retreat into Silesia toward Schweidnitz, a place well-suited to support Austria in the event that she joined the Allies, or from which to advance to the aid of Prussia.

The next day Napoleon moved his main body east toward the river Katzbach. He ordered Oudinot in the direction of Berlin, while Davout was to advance from the lower Elbe. On 28 May, as Davout entered Hamburg, Prussians under Bülow defeated Oudinot near Luckau. Napoleon's own advance east was slowed up by stiff resistance from the Allied rearguard, and had only reached Breslau by 1 June.

On the following day both sides agreed to a 36-hour ceasefire, extended from 4 June by a general armistice. Napoleon withdrew to Dresden. Although some observers have since identified this decision as the source of Napoleon's ultimate downfall, he had sound reasons for agreeing to an armistice. His army was tired, having assumed the offensive and marched several hundred miles, and it had twice inflicted significant, though not decisive, victories on the Allies, in a continuing effort to deliver a final hammerblow. Lack of cavalry had prevented him from exploiting these successes. Despite many weaknesses Napoleon's army had performed remarkably well, but with his supply lines perilously long, his artillery ammunition nearly exhausted, and his casualties equaling those of his opponents, his army now needed a respite in order to recover and regroup. In the political realm, Napoleon also wished to determine and influence the future course of the Emperor Francis, who had by this time established a sizable army abreast of the French right flank.

Both sides extended the armistice to 16 August, enabling the respective armies to rest from the season's campaigning and the commanders to rebuild the wreck of their formations. The Allies benefited most from this pause in hostilities. By the middle of August Napoleon was able to field approximately 440,000 men for the main theater of operations in Germany, and another quarter of a million were stationed in pockets, such as the Bavarian contingent under General Wrede (1767–1838) on the

river Inn. Moreover, the Emperor had amassed over 1,300 guns, thus replacing the numbers lost in Russia. The Allies, on the other hand, had mustered no fewer than 500,000 men for front-line operations, enjoyed an enormous superiority in cavalry, and would soon muster another 350,000 reserve troops.

On the diplomatic front important developments were under way. At Reichenbach on 24 June the Austrian Foreign Minister, Prince Clemens von Metternich (1773–1859), concluded a treaty with Alexander and Frederick William by which Austria assumed the role of armed mediator between Napoleon and those sovereigns. Four terms would be put to the French emperor, whose failure to agree to them would signal Austrian adherence to the Allied camp. The terms required Napoleon to dissolve the

Field Marshal Gebhardt Leberecht von Blücher. A strident Francophobe, Blücher commanded the Prussian forces in 1813–15, proving himself a man of action rather than of intellect. One fellow officer noted that 'His energy was prodigious, he was always on horseback … his eye for ground was excellent, his heroic courage inspired the troops, but … he had little knowledge of strategy, he could not find where he was on a map, and he was incapable of making a plan of campaign or a troop disposition.' (Philip Haythornthwaite)

The battle of Lützen, 2 May 1813. During furious fighting in Ney's sector of the field, General Girard was dismounted and hit twice by musket fire. Spattered in blood, he seized a regimental flag and led his men against massed Prussian artillery, declaring, 'It is here that every brave Frenchman must conquer or die!' On receiving a third bullet wound he passed command to a subordinate, telling him, 'I can do no more.' (AKG, Berlin)

Duchy of Warsaw, permit an enlarged Prussia, restore to Austria her former Illyrian provinces along the Adriatic coast, and re-establish the Hanseatic towns, notably Hamburg, Lübeck, Bremen and Danzig. Napoleon, as was expected, rejected these terms and on 19 July Austria joined the Sixth Coalition, to which Sweden had already been added on 7 July, though the armistice continued in force until the following month.

The autumn campaign

The armistice ended prematurely after 50 days when Austria formally declared war on 12 August. Blücher began to advance from Breslau, in Silesia, on the following day. The truce formally ended on 16 August during which time both sides had been active in raising, training, and shifting troops on a massive scale. Allied forces were organized

into four main armies: Blücher led the Army of Silesia, composed of 95,000 Prussians and Russians, south of Breslau; Bernadotte commanded the Army of the North, consisting of 110,000 Prussians and Swedes at Berlin; Schwarzenberg had 230,000 Austrians in the Army of Bohemia, then massing near the upper Elbe; 60,000 Russians, known as the Army of Poland, were being organized in the rear under General Bennigsen (1745–1826).

All these forces were to fall under the authority of the supreme commander, Schwarzenberg, who soon found his authority undermined and interfered with by the three monarchs accompanying headquarters, together with their staffs, foreign envoys, and others from various countries. Alexander, Francis, and Frederick William had the disconcerting habit of altering Schwarzenberg's orders seemingly by whim:

His Majesty the Tsar of Russia, he wrote to Francis, … *never leaves me alone, not in my headquarters nor on the battlefield … he allows almost every [Russian] general to give advice and suggestions …*

Nevertheless, the Allies formulated a new and promising strategy, called the Trachenberg

Plan, designed to avoid a confrontation with Napoleon's main army and instead concentrate on his subordinates. Results would necessarily be limited, but by these means the Emperor's strength would be gradually diminished. In line with this plan, the Allies decided on 17 August to launch an attack in the direction of Leipzig, conducted from three sides. Meanwhile, news of the victory achieved by the Duke of Wellington (1769–1852) at Vitoria provided a well-timed boost to Allied morale.

Napoleon, with about 400,000 men all told in Germany, did not suffer from the same command and administrative problems facing Schwarzenberg, since he controlled an army which, though it contained foreign contingents, nevertheless was not divided by nationality. Napoleon split his army in two, concentrating about 250,000 men under his personal command along both sides of the Elbe at Dresden, while Oudinot, around Luckau with 120,000 troops, was to make another try against Berlin. Many have criticized Napoleon for his decision to divide his forces and to seek a secondary objective, and this criticism seems largely borne out by

what happened in the course of the next few days, for during that brief period the Emperor would alter his plans several times. First preparing to proceed east for an attack against Blücher, on 18 August he changed direction, moving south toward Zittau in order to threaten Schwarzenberg's rear. Two days later he reverted back to his original march against Blücher, who conformed to the Trachenberg Plan by retreating.

On the following day, 21 August, Napoleon received an appeal from St Cyr at Dresden, calling for assistance against Schwarzenberg, who had switched his main objective from Leipzig to Dresden. Detaching Marshal Macdonald (1765–1840) to keep Blücher in check, Napoleon advanced toward Dresden,

French and Prussian infantry contesting possession of the cemetery at Grossbeeren, 23 August 1813. General Reynier, with a corps of 27,000 men, advanced against the flank of the Prussian main body, seizing the village of Grossbeeren and the heights behind it by late afternoon. The tide soon turned, however, when Bülow arrived with 38,000 troops, smashing through the Saxon contingent to recapture the village and obliging Reynier to withdraw after a failed counterattack. (AKG, Berlin)

only to decide on 23 August that rather than bringing direct support to St Cyr, he must menace the rear of Schwarzenberg's army at Königstein and Pirna. Meanwhile Oudinot had suffered defeat at Grossbeeren on 23 August, and when news of this reached Napoleon's headquarters two days later, together with intelligence reporting that the defense of Dresden was about to collapse, the Emperor again altered his plans, leaving one corps to attack Pirna while pushing the remainder of his forces to the relief of St Cyr.

At Dresden, St Cyr had meanwhile been offering a spirited defense and had ordered several counterattacks, before Napoleon arrived with 70,000 men and threw back the Allied assault on 26 August. At the same time General Vandamme (1770–1830) was in action at Pirna, where he kept Allied reserves occupied while Napoleon concentrated his efforts around Dresden itself. During the night another 50,000 French troops arrived and these, together with Vandamme's diversion, contributed to Napoleon's significant success on the second day of fighting at Dresden. Nevertheless, the victory was tainted when 80,000 men under Macdonald were defeated on the same day at the Katzbach, losing 13,000 killed or drowned, 17,000–20,000 taken prisoner, 150 cannon and two eagles lost. There, in torrential rain, the veteran of Wagram and the Russian campaign had crossed the swollen river and was attacked by the Prussians, who emerged from woods and engaged the French in vicious hand-to-hand fighting, the rain having rendered musket fire impossible. Sword, lance and bayonet accounted for fearful losses and when, together with concentrated artillery fire, Blücher launched 20,000 cavalry, they drove the French down a slope and into the river, where many were drowned and quarter was seldom given to those who survived. French reverses continued elsewhere: Oudinot retreated in the aftermath of Grossbeeren, and the Allies scored a signal triumph at Kulm on 30 August, which not only wiped out Vandamme's command and led to his capture, but enabled Schwarzenberg, then in retreat, to escape. Thus, three of Napoleon's subordinates had lost three battles

in as many days, so canceling out for their emperor the benefits he had accrued at Dresden, where he had defeated an army two and a half times the size of his own.

Pressed on three fronts, French forces also suffered from continuous raids against their communication and supply lines, and morale was falling.

'I have never entertained any hope', wrote a French officer to his wife on 8 September:

that we can withstand so many allied powers, because unfortunately I have noticed among our troops a very feeble degree of enthusiasm, although most of them boast of possessing a great deal of just that quality. Moreover, our soldiers are so small, so weak physically, so young, [and] so inexperienced, that the majority of them give one more cause to fear than to hope.

Lack of training and combat experience and acute shortage of cavalry left Napoleon's army unable either to learn the whereabouts of its enemies or concentrate against them, while the Emperor watched helplessly as his lieutenants were constantly threatened or attacked. Moreover, the mounting pressure imposed by increasing Allied numbers remained a constant source of anxiety for Napoleon, whose decline in health, including depression and lethargy, impaired his effectiveness at a time when the pressure of business most demanded his attention. Napoleon's presence on the battlefield was all the more critical, a fact highlighted in a report to his king by the commander of the Württemberg division of Napoleon's army:

It seems to me that the French generals and officers are sick of the war, and only the Emperor's presence can animate the soldiers … Since the defeats of Macdonald [Katzbach], Vandamme [Kulm], and Ney [Dennewitz] they believe that only the Rhine can afford them any protection against the Cossacks.

With Schwarzenberg beyond his reach over the mountains of Bohemia, Napoleon planned another push toward Berlin beginning on 2 September, and commanded by Ney. Blücher, however, continued his drive against Macdonald, obliging Napoleon on the following day to hold back some of the troops intended for Ney's operations. From Dresden the Emperor proceeded east to reform Macdonald's formations, but Blücher again eluded the main French army by retiring east of Bautzen. In the midst of planning to renew his operations against Berlin, Napoleon had again to divert his attention to a new threat, this time from Schwarzenberg, whose army re-crossed the Elbe and detached a force under Barclay de Tolly toward Dresden. The Emperor had little option but to respond, moving his main body toward Kulm, behind Barclay's rear, but Schwarzenberg refused to give battle and rapidly withdrew back across the Elbe. The French abandoned their pursuit on 10 September, and in the meantime to the north Ney had been forced to retreat from Dennewitz.

A series of threats during the next two weeks continued to rob Napoleon of the initiative. He could not ignore Schwarzenberg's renewed diversionary movements in the direction of Dresden, and he was unable to reinforce Ney's drive on Berlin until that threat had been dealt with. There were further problems to the north: Bernadotte with 80,000 men would soon be at the Elbe, while Blücher once again struck at Macdonald's exhausted men.

By late September the strain on French forces was becoming critical. Their numbers had been reduced by 200,000 men since the middle of August, the shortage of supplies was reaching a state of crisis, and the Allies continued to keep their opponents marching and countermarching in a fruitless attempt to hold back superior numbers threatening from more directions than available numbers could withstand. This critical state of affairs persuaded Napoleon to withdraw all his field forces west of the Elbe, and when the troops began to march on 24 September French garrisons further east were left to fend for themselves as best they could, well aware that all hope for direct relief from their emperor had vanished.

While Napoleon was moving west, in the north Bernadotte was at the Elbe, across which he began to establish bridgeheads. On the following day Blücher began marching to support him, himself relieved by Bennigsen's arrival. Troops under Bernadotte and Blücher combined to form 140,000 men and these, together with 180,000 under Schwarzenberg and Bennigsen, would now march toward Leipzig, a city of great strategic importance as a communications link with the Rhine and France beyond. On his march to reach Bernadotte, Blücher's 60,000 men fought a number of minor clashes before reaching Wartenberg, on the Elbe, on 3 October. Overpowering the weak corps under Bertrand before crossing the river on 4 October, Blücher proceeded to Delitsch, about 20 miles (30 km) north of Leipzig, with Bernadotte marching parallel.

General Dominique Joseph Vandamme. A veteran of the French Revolutionary Wars and every subsequent campaign fought outside Spain, Vandamme was noted for corruption and an eye for loot. Nevertheless, he possessed the aggressiveness and energy required of a successful field commander. During operations in Germany he achieved a minor victory at Pirna before losing more than half his command and falling into Prussian hands at Kulm. During the Waterloo campaign he led a corps at Ligny and Wavre. (Philip Haythornthwaite)

The battle of Kulm, 30 August 1813. Another Allied victory achieved over one of Napoleon's subordinates, as part of the Trachenberg Plan. Despite enjoying a 2-to-1 numerical superiority over Marshal Oudinot, Bernadotte contemplated abandoning Berlin, a course of action roundly condemned by von Bülow, who declared that while the Swedes could do as they pleased, the Prussians would attack. They did so with enthusiasm, capturing Vandamme and thousands of his troops. (AKG, Berlin)

By this time Napoleon had firmly established himself in Leipzig with nearly 250,000 men, and could easily outnumber either of the Allied armies en route to engage him. Napoleon now took the initiative: appointing Murat with 43,000 men to oppose an attack from the south, and corps under Mouton and St Cyr, respectively, to hold Dresden, the Emperor marched north on 7 October with 150,000 men and attacked Blücher at Düben. The attempt at surprise failed, and Blücher managed to retire west to the Saale. Frustrated in his attempts to monitor Allied movements owing to a shortage of cavalry, Napoleon was left to proceed north with caution toward Dresden, where Bernadotte was based.

But if Napoleon was moving slowly in one direction, Schwarzenberg, whose troops after reinforcement numbered 240,000, was advancing even more slowly toward Leipzig. Murat delayed him at Borna on 10 October, and two days later Ney blocked part of Bernadotte's forces from crossing the river Mulde near Dessau. Nevertheless, the various Allied forces were now sufficiently close to one another to cooperate in an attack against Leipzig. The future was looking bleak for the French, prompting one sergeant of dragoons to admit that the war was no longer to defend the Empire, but to keep the Allies away from France herself. 'I'll tell you one thing,' he wrote on 12 October:

in a month we shall be on the banks of the Rhine. The vengeance of the nations we have conquered, trampled upon and plundered, will invade France in order to make a wilderness of the country. To prevent this happening is the only reason a right-minded Frenchman can have for bearing arms.

On 13 October Wittgenstein marched from the south to reconnoiter, while on the

Prussian *Landwehr* cavalry charging at Dennewitz, 6 September 1813. While approaching Berlin, Ney, with 55,000 men, attacked 80,000 Prussians led by von Bülow, while a further 30,000 Swedes remained in reserve under Bernadotte. At a critical point in the fighting, Ney's Saxons deserted, leaving a massive gap in his line through which rode a large body of Prussian cavalry, severing Ney's command and forcing him to retire to Torgau. (AKG, Berlin)

following day Napoleon, aware that he had failed to halt the Allies' approach from the north, ordered all his forces to assemble in defense of Leipzig. His troops were now in a dreadful condition, as a colonel in the Old Guard noted on 15 October:

From the time the regiment left its cantonments on 6 October, the soldiers had not received a single ounce of bread. On this march, made wretched by bad roads and bad weather, the only issue of rations was a little rice and meat. So one can easily picture the state that the army was in and the difference between units which went short of nothing and those which had just enough

food to avoid dying of hunger. To the shortages of food was added the lack of shoes. One saw a great many troops walking barefoot in the mud and water, their feet and legs cut and bleeding. This state of affairs made any officer weep who had not lost all feelings of humanity.

A major cavalry engagement took place at Liebertwolkwitz on 14 October, with no decisive outcome, but the main action took place over three days: 16–18 October. The contest for the village of Möckern exemplifies the bitterness of the fighting. There, Marmont's men struggled against the Prussians, with the village changing hands several times throughout the first day of the fighting. Yorck's men, who contested every house and street, could only be dislodged in dreadful hand-to-hand fighting. By dusk, the Prussians were left in control of the place, albeit choked with the dead and dying. Yorck lost 8,000 of his 21,000 men, and the French about the same number – making this 'battle within a battle' the most costly, as a

Leipzig, 19 October 1813. The battle having been lost, a large French column (background) attempts to evacuate the city while units of the beleaguered rearguard (left foreground) defend a barricade against Prussian *Landwehr*. As ordinary infantry could seldom fire more than one or two rounds a minute, close-quarter fighting like this sometimes required use of the bayonet or musket-butt. (Philip Haythornthwaite)

proportion of the numbers engaged, of any combat of the Napoleonic Wars. All the while, Ney, with 15,000 men, had crisscrossed the battlefield, trying to support separate sectors, but in the end failed to reinforce either of them. Savage street-fighting was common during the battle – Möckern was far from unique – with many sections of the city and surrounding villages passing into the possession of one side and then the other, often with no quarter being offered or received. General Langeron, a French émigré fighting for the Russians, retook the village of Schönefeld twice on the third day of the battle:

I believed the position was assured, and went forward of the village to establish a chain of outposts. At this moment Ney … launched against me so unexpected an attack, and so impetuous and well directed, that I was unable to withstand it. Five columns, advancing at the charge and with fixed bayonets, rushed at the village and at my troops, who were still scattered and whom I was trying to re-form. They were overthrown and forced to retire in a hurry. I was swept along by the fugitives, but I really cannot

blame their sudden retreat because it was impossible to hold out, and I must confess that they moved as fast as I could manage.

… Fortunately I still had considerable reserves, and after letting the regiments which had been expelled from Schönefeld pass through the gaps between them, I soon did to the enemy what he had done to me, because my columns were in good order and his troops were by this time scattered.

Nevertheless, the bitter fighting around Schönefeld carried on for the course of the day until, with their reserves exhausted, the French conceded the place to the Allies. But the suffering did not end there: when fire broke out those who had fallen wounded inside the battered structures or who had crawled into them in search of safety instead found themselves trapped. One anonymous account described this dreadful scene thus:

The struggle for Probstheida, 18 October 1813. On the third day's fighting around Leipzig, Barclay de Tolly halted near this village, doggedly held by Macdonald's troops. By nightfall Probstheida had changed hands several times, leaving the streets and houses clogged with Russian and French casualties, but with Macdonald still in possession. (AKG, Berlin)

Battle of Leipzig (first day), 16 October 1813

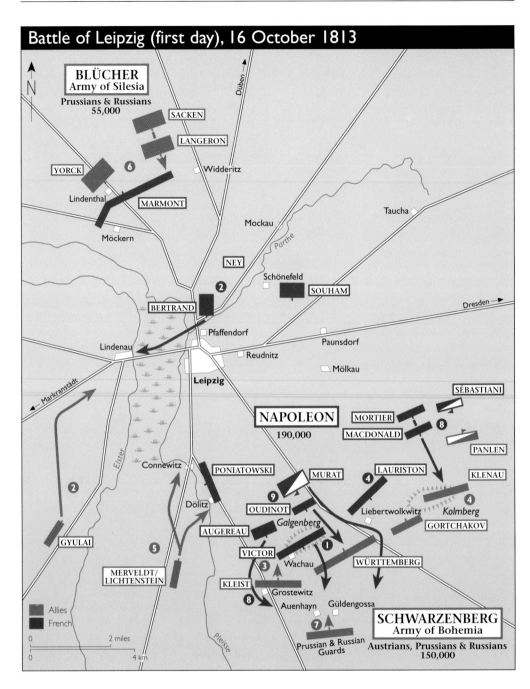

Many wounded on both sides were burnt to death and in the manor-farm all the cattle perished, even the huge black bull ... Maddened by all the firing and yelling, and by burns, the bull had broken loose ... and run ... against the attacking Russians so irresistibly that on his own he scattered an entire column. The burning church-tower made common cause with the raging bull to defeat the Russians. It collapsed and buried a large number of these soldiers beneath its ruins ... the noise and shouting of the troops, the sound of artillery and small-arms fire, the landing and explosion of shells, the howling, moaning and lowing of human beings and cattle, the whimpering and calls for help from the wounded and those who lay half-buried *alive under the masonry, blazing planks and beams was hideous. The smoke, dust and fumes made the day so dark that nobody could tell what time of day it was.*

One of the most dramatic events of the third day was the sudden defection of the Saxons and their guns, followed soon thereafter by the Württemberger cavalry. For the French, retreat was now vital, and on the morning of 19 October Napoleon's troops began to cross the River Elster, protected by a strong rearguard. On seeing this, the Allies, and Blücher in particular, launched a furious attack on the defenders and the city in a determined bid to prevent a French escape. Only one bridge then spanned the river, with a lone sergeant of engineers left with responsibility to ignite the charge on the appearance of opposing forces. The sergeant interpreted his orders literally: when nothing more than a small body of Prussian riflemen appeared on the opposite river bank, he blew the bridge – prematurely – cutting Napoleon's army in two and inflicting more damage on his remaining forces than the previous three days' fighting. Three army corps totaling

37,000 men, including all their artillery, as well as approximately 20,000 walking wounded and others, 30 generals and two marshals, were left stranded on the wrong side of the Elster, there to be captured or killed in the fighting.

Marshal Macdonald barely reached safety: 'I escaped … with a firm resolve not to fall alive into the hands of the enemy, preferring to shoot or drown myself,' he wrote in his memoirs. Encountering a ramshackle 'bridge' originally fashioned from two trees, doors, shutters and planks, but now reduced merely to the trees, Macdonald had no option but to attempt a crossing, as he later recorded in his memoirs:

It was my only chance; I made up my mind and risked it. I got off my horse with great difficulty, owing to the crowd, and there I was, one foot on either trunk, and the abyss below me. A high wind was blowing … I had already made three-quarters of my way across, when some men determined to follow me; their unsteady feet caused the trunks to shake, and I fell into the water. I could fortunately touch the bottom, but the bank was steep, the soil loose and greasy; I vainly struggled to reach the shore.

Practically everyone else was left behind or drowned (including Marshal Poniatowski) in the effort of crossing. Macdonald himself was powerless to assist those left on the opposite bank:

On the other side of the Elster the firing continued; it suddenly ceased. Our unhappy troops were crowded together on the river-bank; whole companies plunged into the water and were carried away; cries of despair rose on all sides. The men perceived me. Despite the noise and tumult, I distinctly heard these words: 'Monsieur le Maréchal, save your men! Save your children!' I could do nothing for them! Overcome by rage, indignation, fury, I wept!

Until the disaster at the Elster the battle had remained a drawn affair. Yet in an instant it had been converted into a great Allied victory. Casualties were enormous, the Allies losing approximately 55,000 killed and wounded, while the French suffered 38,000 casualties between 16 and 18 October, in addition to the more than 50,000 men captured the next day. Another 5,000 German troops had defected during the battle. Practically every piece of French equipment was lost, including over 300 guns. In Leipzig itself, one resident noted how the city had been 'transformed into one vast hospital, 56 edifices being devoted to that purpose alone. The number of sick and wounded amounted to 36,000. Of these a large proportion died, but their places were soon supplied by the many wounded who had been left in the adjacent villages.'

Prince Schwarzenberg at the battle of Leipzig, announcing victory to the Allied sovereigns: Tsar Alexander of Russia, King Frederick William of Prussia, and the Emperor Francis of Austria. Commander-in-Chief of the Allied armies from August 1813 to April 1814, Schwarzenberg found his duties continuously interfered with by these crowned heads and their respective staff officers. 'It is really inhuman what I have to tolerate and bear,' he bitterly complained, 'surrounded as I am by weaklings, fools of all kinds, eccentric project-makers, intriguers, blockheads, gossips and fault-finders.' (AKG, Berlin)

Leipzig was the largest and one of the most decisive battles of the Napoleonic Wars. French political influence in Germany collapsed, and physical control evaporated as the French armies hastily made for the Rhine via the supply lines of Frankfurt and Mainz. Napoleon's German allies had all defected: Bavaria before, and Saxony and Württemberg during, the battle. Saxony, like the Duchy of Warsaw before it, was occupied by Allied troops, with the brief exception of Dresden, whose French garrison finally surrendered on 11 November. The remaining states of the Confederation of the Rhine quickly broke away or were lost to French influence. General van der Gelder, the commander of one of the German brigades of the *Grande Armée*, was not surprised when the troops had finally had enough:

The French were to complain loudly when their allies deserted them during the famous days of Leipzig, but I venture to ask them whether they would tolerate humiliations and bad treatment from allies more powerful than themselves, and whether they would not turn against men who

devastated their country, burning and plundering
everything, beating and raping without any
redress being made and oblivious to every
complaint. Well! That is what the Saxons and
other Germans had been suffering for years.

The Allies did not offer a vigorous pursuit
and the French retreat carried on largely
unhindered until it reached Erfurt on
23 October. A week later General Wrede,
with his Bavarian force of 60,000, sought to
block the French march at Hanau. There, on
30 October, he foolishly deployed his men
with their backs to a river with only a single
bridge by which to make their escape if
circumstances so required. By resting one of
his flanks against woods light enough to
permit the passage of artillery, Wrede found
himself under fire from the elite artillery of
the Imperial Guard, which with 50 guns
wrecked havoc in his ranks. Then, Marbot
recalled in his memoirs:

… just as a puff of wind drove the smoke
away, the Chasseurs [à Cheval] of the Guard
appeared. At the sight of the Chasseurs'
bearskins the Bavarian infantry recoiled in
consternation. Wishing to check the disorder at
any cost, General Wrede made all the cavalry at
his disposal charge our guns, and in a moment
the battery was surrounded by a cloud of
horsemen … Numbers would, however, have
triumphed but that – at the Emperor's order –
the whole of Sébastiani's cavalry and that of the
[Imperial] Guard … all dashed furiously on the
enemy, killing a great number and scattering the
rest. Then, flying upon the squares of Bavarian
infantry, they broke them with heavy loss and
the routed Bavarian army fled towards the bridge
and the town of Hanau.

Wrede's disastrous folly cost him
6,000 men. Napoleon, with approximately
70,000 men and another 40,000 stragglers, was
therefore enabled to reach Frankfurt, only
20 miles (30 km) from the Rhine, on
2 November. Within four days, re-equipped
with new weapons and uniforms from the
magazine at Erfurt, the French crossed the
Rhine at Mainz, and now stood safely – at

least for the time being, on native soil.
However, about 100,000 of their comrades had
been abandoned in Germany – the corps led
by Davout on the lower Elbe, plus many small
forces occupying towns and cities throughout
Germany. Isolated, outnumbered and in most
cases besieged, all of them surrendered, mostly
unconditionally, over the following few weeks
with the exception of the Hamburg garrison,
where Davout steadfastly refused to give in.
With their capture, total French losses in the
autumn campaign had reached about
400,000, and this, combined with the loss of
all German territory beyond the Rhine,
rendered the Leipzig campaign nothing short
of a catastrophe for Napoleon.

The situation may be summed up thus: in
the past two years the Emperor had
commanded forces numbering in excess of
400,000 men. Twice he had ended the
campaigns with fewer than 70,000. Allied
armies numbering 345,000 men were poised
to invade from the east, while another Allied
army of about 125,000 men under
Wellington was already in south-west France,
opposed by 100,000 troops under Marshals
Soult (1769–1851) and Suchet (1770–1826).
With only 80,000 men to defend the east of
the country, and spread across 300 miles
(482 km), France now braced herself for a
crisis not experienced since the early years of
the Revolutionary Wars, two decades before.

The campaign in France, 1814

Following the overwhelming Allied victory
at Leipzig and the retreat of the French to
the Rhine, the main operations in 1814
would shift from Germany to eastern France,
where Napoleon could not even muster
100,000 men to oppose the Allied armies
approaching the Rhine at the end of
1813 with a combined strength of over
300,000 men. French armies on the two
other fronts also faced dire prospects. In
Italy, the Austrian general Bellagarde opened
hostilities against Eugène, and in south-west
France Wellington continued to press French
forces there. In Paris, as well as in the

Battle of Leipzig (third day), 18 October 1813

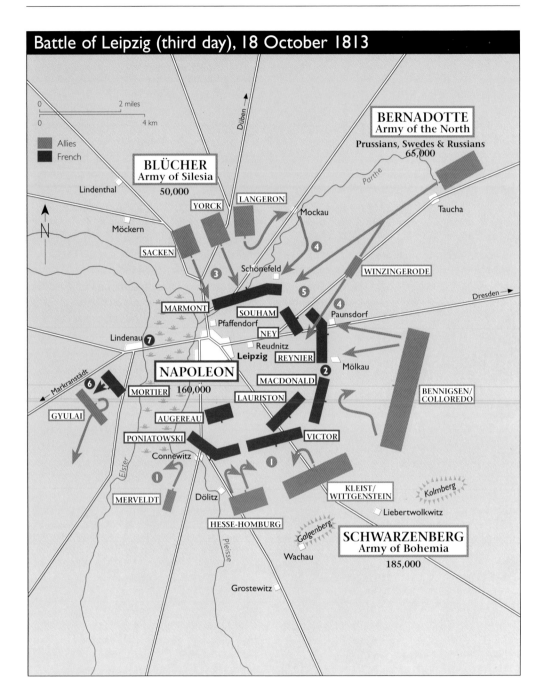

countryside, political uneasiness with the regime and general war-weariness began to exacerbate an increasingly dire military situation.

Napoleon recognized that an acute shortage of men posed his greatest short-term problem. The campaigns of 1812 and 1813 had cost him nearly a million men, and there were no simple means of replacing even a fraction of these – particularly with the loss (mostly by defection) of his vassal states east of the Rhine. Napoleon wrongly assumed that the Allies on the Rhine would require several months in which to rest and prepare for the next campaign; this would give him time to tap every possible source of manpower to raise new armies. But his target, 900,000 men, was grossly unrealistic. On 5 November, Cambacérès (1753–1824), the Emperor's chief executive, informed the Emperor that the immediate levy of 140,000 men could be met,

LEFT

1. 7.00 am General assault by Schwarzenberg. Stiff resistance halts Allied progress. Hesse-Homburg takes Dölitz, while Poniatowski denies Connewitz from Merveldt. Victor repulses Kleist and Wittgenstein.
2. Macdonald keeps Colloredo in check, but reinforcements from Bennigsen enable him to seize Holzhausen. Reynier retains Mölkau and Paunsdorf.
3. Blücher detaches Langeron to assist Bernadotte, then captures Pfaffendorff, before his advance founders. Despite reaching as far as Reudnitz, Prussians are driven out by reinforcements sent by Napoleon.
4. Around mid-day Bernadotte's advance guard links up with Langeron, who attacks Ney at Schönefeld. Winzingerode advances on Paunsdorf, meeting up with Bennigsen, so closing the gap between the Armies of Silesia and Bohemia. Bennigsen resumes attack. Reynier's Saxons and Württembergers defect. Paunsdorf falls to the Allies.
5. Temporarily retaking Paunsdorf, Ney nevertheless is forced back by sheer numbers. Prussians penetrate to Reudnitz. Langeron, in a see-saw action, finally captures Schönefeld.
6. As Allies force French back into Leipzig, Mortier's Young Guard pushes Gyulai back and clears way for westward retreat.
7. Napoleon orders general retreat at 2.00 am on 19 October. Elster bridge at Lindenau prematurely blown, stranding thousands on the wrong side.

but not without employing new methods. Nearly 80,000 were already available, but as for the shortfall, he confessed that:

… we can no longer think in terms of unmarried men, since the last available conscript in this category has already been called up. There is little evidence that we can count on the willingness to volunteer of married men, for most of them have only contracted marriage in order not to join up, and the price of substitutes is so high that such a measure as purchasing replacements would be impracticable, unless we recruit married men.

Rather than risk 'certain problems' and 'uncertain results' by calling up earlier classes of men and those married but without children, Cambacérès decided to transfer 100,000 men from the National Guard, with

BELOW Imperial Guard infantry, 1814. Not only the élite of Napoleon's army, but one of the most famous military bodies in the history of warfare, the Imperial Guard also included cavalry, artillery and engineers. The infantry was traditionally retained as a reserve and rarely saw action on the battlefield until 1814, when desperate circumstances demanded their deployment in the front line. At Waterloo Napoleon was obliged to commit some units of the Guard to defend his vulnerable right flank against the Prussians, while he ordered others against Wellington's wavering center. (Philip Haythornthwaite)

no exemptions for married men. The sources of manpower were rapidly drying up, but if a shortage of men posed insuperable problems, at least Allied indecision and bickering offered Napoleon precious time.

At the same time, Napoleon employed diplomacy to placate his enemies and curry favor with public opinion abroad, particularly in Italy and Spain. He cynically restored Pope Pius VII (1742–1823) to Rome in an attempt to retain the loyalty of Italians, while with Ferdinand VII of Spain (1784–1833) he concluded the Treaty of Valençay, in a feeble attempt to terminate the Franco–Spanish conflict.

It is appropriate here to pause and consider the Allies' political and strategic aims and examine how these affected the conduct of their military operations. Recovery of northern Italy was Austria's prime objective, not the destruction of France, for Marie-Louise, Francis's daughter, remained Empress. Britain wanted to re-establish the balance of power on the Continent, and would not countenance a gravely weakened France. Bernadotte, Crown Prince of Sweden but a Frenchman by birth, was extremely unwilling to attack his native country – a reluctance almost certainly a consequence of his wish to succeed Napoleon on the throne. On the other hand, Alexander wanted vengeance for the invasion of his country, and Frederick William, as Alexander's junior partner, was prepared to support the Tsar – not least because of the vociferous and belligerent attitudes of men like Blücher, who had scores to settle for the humiliations Prussia had suffered in 1806 and for her subsequent partition and occupation.

Allied leaders gathered at Frankfurt in November and on the 16th agreed to offer negotiating terms to the French, with what France considered her 'natural frontiers' (the Rhine, the Alps and the Pyrenees) as the principal basis. In the meantime the three Allied armies poised on the Rhine stood down. With no intention of adhering to these terms, Napoleon first proposed the establishment of an international congress as a forum for negotiation and then, on 30 November,

disingenuously accepted the peace proposals. Allied policy had, however, changed by this time, with the members of the coalition demanding the more restricted borders of 1792, which excluded much of the Rhineland and the whole of the Low Countries. Such terms were deliberately designed to be rejected, and in late December the short hiatus in military activity ceased with a renewed Allied offensive into eastern France conducted from three directions. Just prior to entering France herself, the Allies issued a proclamation explaining that the conflict was directed more specifically against the Emperor:

We do not make war on France, but we are casting off a yoke which your Government imposed on our countries. We had hoped to have found peace before touching your soil: we now go to find it there.

One division of Austrians entered Switzerland unopposed, while the Bavarians under Wrede passed the Rhine on 22 December and began to besiege Hunigen. On the northern front, Prussians under Bülow and a small British force under Sir Thomas Graham (1748–1843) marched into Holland as a prelude to taking Antwerp, occupying the remainder of Belgium and invading France. On the central front, Blücher began crossing the Rhine on 29 December between Koblenz and Mannheim at the head of 100,000 Prussians, with the intention of occupying Napoleon's main army as the other Allied armies approached.

On 1 January the southern wing of the Allied offensive, consisting of 200,000 men under Schwarzenberg, began its march toward Colmar on the upper Rhine, with the intention of threatening Napoleon's right flank and linking up with Allied troops moving north from Spain and Italy. Far to the east, Bernadotte, with a large combined Russo–Swedish army, remained behind in Germany to watch Davout's corps isolated at Hamburg and other smaller French garrisons. Napoleon could only muster around 67,000 men distributed along the whole border stretching from Switzerland to the

Dutch coast. The Imperial Guard was under strength and only about 30,000 partly trained militia stood in reserve. Recruitment yields had fallen drastically short of actual need, and the army was desperately short of weapons, equipment, and experienced NCOs.

Napoleon's diplomatic efforts, meanwhile, failed entirely: Ferdinand of Spain renounced the Treaty of Valençay, ensuring that Wellington would continue operations in south-west France. Murat, as king of Naples, joined the Allies on 11 January, and Denmark followed suit three days later. Even at home the Emperor now began to face opposition and conspiracies were brewing for a Bourbon restoration. No less than the Foreign Minister himself, Talleyrand, had begun secret talks with the exiled Louis XVIII (1755–1824), then in England.

While his forces in the east of the country faced impossible odds against the Allied advance, Napoleon remained in the capital trying to cope with increasingly complex political matters at a time when his troops could not offer adequate resistance without their emperor in the field. To the south, Marshal Victor (1764–1841), defending the border there, abandoned Strasbourg and Nancy without firing a shot, and Marmont with 16,000 men, was pushed back toward Metz, which he reached on 13 January. Within four days both corps, together with Ney's contingent of the Young Guard, had retreated across the Meuse. Although Napoleon shifted Marshal Mortier (1768–1835) and the Imperial Guard to this sector, they were unable to prevent Blücher's Prussians from pushing across the Meuse on 22 January.

On the following day his advance guard crossed the Marne, while at the same time Schwarzenberg, held up for six days by the new proposals, was nearing Bar-sur-Aube, only 25 miles (40 km) to the southwest. Mortier, together with part of the corps under General Gérard (1773–1852), offered a stiff rearguard defense there on 24 January, but were unable to halt the Allies and withdrew west toward Troyes. At the same time, on the distant northern front, Bülow and Graham were making steady progress against Macdonald's corps of 15,000 men, who were forced out of Liège and obliged to withdraw toward the Meuse.

Apart from their forces in the far north, the Allies had 200,000 men marching on Paris, opposed by only 85,000 French. Although the capital's defenses were badly in need of repair and suspicions abounded that treason was rife, the Emperor was prepared to fight to the end. Having placed his brother Joseph (1768–1844) in charge of the government, Napoleon left the capital on 25 January to resume direct command of the troops at the front.

He arrived in the area south-east of Paris on the following day. This was generally open ground – otherwise ideal terrain over which the Allied advance could proceed – except that it was laced by numerous rivers such as the Meuse and Seine, which offered obstacles to the approach to Paris if the bridges were strongly held or destroyed. Recognizing that his forces could not survive the strain of a major action – whatever the outcome – Napoleon decided to employ a strategy of rapid marches that could take advantage of internal lines of communication without the limitations imposed by supply wagons. Freed from these constraints he could concentrate on and destroy in turn small portions of the Allied armies operating in isolation from their main bodies.

Napoleon first chose to strike at Blücher, who was then moving up in two columns sufficiently distant from one another to be vulnerable. The Emperor failed to make contact at St Dizier on 27 January, and at Brienne, two days later, he achieved only a minor victory. He pursued, but Blücher turned and in a surprise counterattack at La Rothière on 1 February inflicted a sound defeat that seriously damaged French morale. Poor training was now graphically evident. During the action Marmont asked a young infantryman why he was not discharging his weapon, to which the recruit replied: 'I would, sir, if I knew how!' On this, the marshal dismounted and instructed him.

Amazingly, Napoleon still retained the option of concluding a peace which would permit him to retain his throne. The proposal had come from the Allies on 29 January, and on 3 February a conference convened at Châtillon-sur-Seine. At the same time Napoleon's troops stood on the defensive along the Seine near Troyes, while Marmont received orders to retake Arcis-sur-Aube.

BELOW Having rejected a generous Allied peace offer, Napoleon opted to fight under increasingly dire circumstances. Heavily outnumbered and facing opponents on several fronts, he had no real chance of ejecting them from home soil. While he still retained a quarter of a million men under arms, many of these were poorly-trained and recently recruited, while the Allies could deploy more than double this number, including over 100,000 men in the south under Wellington. Bernadotte, approaching from Holland, Blücher, from Lorraine, and Schwarzenberg, from Switzerland, led another 300,000 between them. While the campaign of 1814 demonstrated that Napoleon had not lost his tactical genius, the sheer number of his opponents and the poor quality of his own forces would ultimately tell.

Encouraged by their success at La Rothière, Schwarzenberg and Blücher pushed on up the Seine and the Marne toward Paris, but suffered a succession of minor reverses in the process. Marmont succeeded in recapturing Arcis-sur- Aube on 3 February, cavalry under General Grouchy (1766–1847) blocked a Russian advance near Troyes, and, to the

RIGHT Fighting took place in bitter cold and snow began to fall around 1.00 pm, when Blücher opened his attack. Württemberg (12,000 men) seized wooded high ground around La Giberie, but was then ejected. The main attack took place on the plain in front of La Rothière, where Gyulai (15,000), Sacken (20,000), and Olssufiev (5,000), despite overwhelming numbers, proved unable to break the French line, consisting of Gérard (5,000), Victor (15,000), Marmont (18,000), and Ney (16,000). To the west, Wrede, with 25,000, engaged Marmont at about 5.00 pm, forcing him back, but failing to defeat him. Heavy winds and flurries brought the fighting to an end, narrowly saving Napoleon from disaster. The Emperor had no choice but to withdraw the following day or risk being surrounded as a consequence of massive Allied numerical superiority.

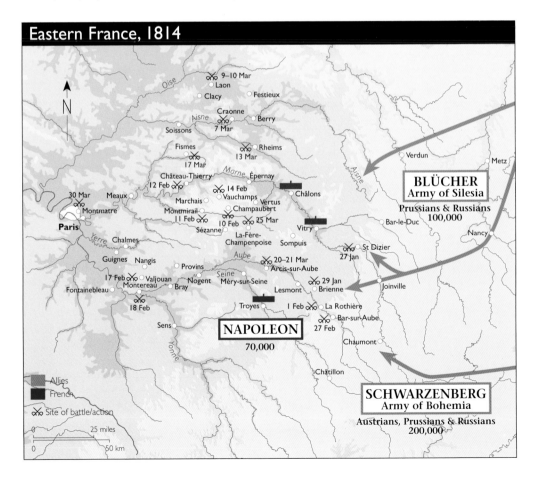

Eastern France, 1814

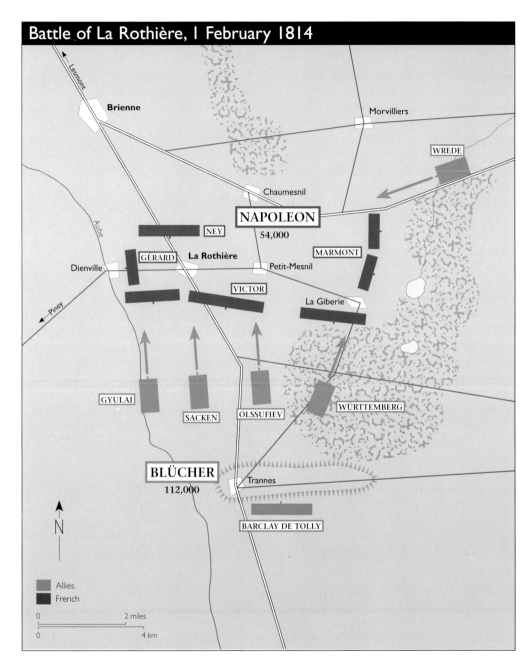

Battle of La Rothière, 1 February 1814

Lesmont

Brienne

Morvilliers

WREDE

Chaumesnil

NAPOLEON
54,000

NEY

Aube

GÉRARD

La Rothière

MARMONT

Dienville

Petit-Mesnil

Piney

VICTOR

La Giberie

GYULAI

SACKEN

OLSSUFIEV

WÜRTTEMBERG

BLÜCHER
112,000

Trannes

N

BARCLAY DE TOLLY

Allies
French

0   2 miles

0   4 km

---

north, the French held Yorck's advance in check at Vitry. Also, at Sens, on the Yonne, a body of Cossacks were driven off. These minor setbacks persuaded the already cautious Schwarzenberg to slow his advance, concerned as he was about intelligence of a new assembly of French troops at Lyon under Marshal Augereau (1757–1816). Blücher, on the other hand, made all speed up the Marne for Paris,

brushing aside the weak contingents seeking to oppose his progress.

At first Napoleon intended to strike at Schwarzenberg, but when he at last concluded on 5 February that Blücher intended to capture the capital itself and that only Macdonald's under-strength corps blocked his path, he concentrated what forces he could for a rapid march to Nogent. Mortier, in the meantime, launched a sortie from Troyes on 6 February, striking Schwarzenberg's right flank and sending him retreating back to Bar-sur-Aube. When Mortier returned to Nogent on 7 February, French forces there numbered approximately 70,000.

On 6 February Napoleon received reports of widespread panic in Paris, together with word that the Prussians had captured Brussels, and that Allied representatives at Châtillon-sur-Seine would accept no negotiated peace short of limiting France to her pre-1792 borders. Napoleon spent 7 February in solitude to consider his next move: by evening he had determined to carry on the war, concentrating his first efforts against Blücher. On 9 February, intelligence reports indicated the Prussian commander's position to be about 15 miles (25 km) east, near Montmirail. Having left Victor and Oudinot with 34,000 men to defend the bridges on the Seine from Schwarzenberg, and having left Macdonald, positioned north of the Marne near Epernay with 18,000 men, to watch Yorck, Napoleon marched a force of 30,000 eastward to Champaubert.

By 9 February Schwarzenberg had proceeded as far as Troyes, but the Allies failed to coordinate simultaneous movements up the Marne by Blücher, Yorck, and Kleist, all of whom struggled with impaired communications caused by melting snow and the onset of heavy rain. By spreading his force of 50,000 men too widely in an attempt to envelop the French around Sézanne, Blücher and his subordinates fell victim to a series of some of Napoleon's most impressive victories.

The first came at Champaubert on 10 February, where Napoleon's force of 30,000 overwhelmed 5,000 Russians under General Olssufiev whom Blücher had detached to operate in the area. On the following day the Emperor struck at Montmirail, defeating a Prussian corps under Sacken before Blücher could complete his attempts at regrouping his scattered forces. On 12 February the French were victorious again at Château-Thierry, though at the same time Macdonald was unable to prevent the Allies from forcing a passage of the Marne. On 14 February Blücher

launched a counterattack at Vauchamps, but was repulsed. All told, what became known as the Six Days' Campaign cost the Allies 20,000 men. Nevertheless, although Napoleon's successes raised French morale, they failed to have a significant effect on the Allies, who brought up 30,000 Russians under Winzingerode to join Blücher's army at Châlons.

To the south, Schwarzenberg was meanwhile pushing west toward Guignes and Chalmes on the river Yerre, driving before him the combined army under Oudinot, Victor and Macdonald. By the middle of the month the Allies were within 20 miles (30 km) of Paris. Panic once again gripped the capital. Schwarzenberg, however, ordered a halt to assess the risks to his flanks. No sooner had he decided to withdraw than Napoleon pounced on and routed his advance guard at Valjouan on 17 February, and on the following day the Emperor defeated Schwarzenberg again at Montereau.

Schwarzenberg's reverse led him to revert back to his cautious strategy, while at the same time it emboldened Napoleon to renew his demand, despite the suspension of peace talks, for the restoration of the 'natural frontiers' as the basis for peace. Circumstances soon obliged him to modify his demand: unable to pursue Schwarzenberg to Troyes because of damage to the bridges across this stretch of the Seine, and aware by 21 February that the main Allied forces were concentrating at Méry-sur-Seine, Napoleon reverted once again to peace terms based on the frontiers of 1792. The offer was rejected, for Francis had already decided to carry on fighting as a result of entreaties from Alexander and Lord Castlereagh, the British Foreign Secretary, not to compromise when total victory appeared to be within reach.

On 22 February the Allies endorsed Schwarzenberg's continued retreat, and despite Blücher's objections, ordered him to withdraw. This denied Napoleon, now reinforced to 74,000 troops near Troyes, the major engagement he had hoped for. The Allies held another summit on 25 February at Bar-sur-Aube, which ordered Schwarzenberg back still further, though he was to advance to Blücher's aid if Napoleon threatened that commander. Blücher's renewed push against Paris had begun the previous day, enabling him to engage Marmont and Mortier near Meaux before proceeding north of the Marne beginning on 1 March. Without bridging equipment Napoleon was unable to pursue the Prussian commander-in-chief, who crossed the Aisne near Soissons with the bulk of his forces in order to link them with those of Winzingerode and Bülow, whose combined strength now exceeded 100,000 men. Quite apart from this overwhelming numerical superiority, Napoleon simply could not be in all places at all times and, taking advantage of this fact, Schwarzenberg resumed his march toward Bar-sur-Aube on 26 February, pushing Macdonald, in temporary command of this sector, toward Nogent, which he reached on 5 March.

Meanwhile, at an historic meeting convened at Chaumont, the Allies belatedly agreed to fight on until final victory, thus ensuring that Austria did not leave the alliance and conclude a separate peace. Castlereagh, fearing that months of careful diplomacy were about to crumble in the face of temporary French successes and bickering and recrimination between Alexander and Francis, had issued an appeal, calling on Austria and Russia to settle their differences for the sake of the common objective. 'I feel it more than ever necessary,' he had written on 18 February:

to conjure you and your colleagues at headquarters not to suffer yourselves to descend from the substance of your peace. You owe it, such as you have announced it, to the enemy, to yourselves, and to Europe, and you will now more than ever make a fatal sacrifice both of moral and political impression, if under the pressure of those slight reverses which are incident to war, and some embarrassments in your council which I should hope are at an end, the great edifice of peace was suffered to be disfigured in its proportions. Recollect what your military position is … If we act with military and political prudence, how can France resist a just peace demanded by 600,000 warriors? Let her, if she dare, and the day

you … declare the fact to the French nation, rest assured Bonaparte is subdued … There can be in good sense but one interest among the [Allied] Powers: namely, to end nobly the great work they have conducted so near to its close.

If the Russians and Austrians were at odds with one another, it was nevertheless clear that the Prussians and French were eager for a fight. Having ordered Marmont to join him from Meaux, Napoleon rapidly crossed the Aisle at Berry-au-Bac on 6 March en route to Laon. Blücher sprung a trap for French forces near Craonne on the same night, leading to fighting on the following day. A few days later, on 9–10 March, another struggle took place, at Laon, from which Napoleon barely managed to withdraw intact.

By now French forces were under great pressure elsewhere. In the south-west, Wellington continued to exert pressure on Soult and Suchet, while in Italy Eugène was faring equally badly. On the north-eastern frontier, Maison had withdrawn to Lille, and French garrisons across eastern France were cut off from all possible relief. Further into the interior, Augereau failed to get clear of Lyons and was forced back on 9 March, while on 12 March the authorities in Bordeaux hoisted the fleur-de-lis. In Paris itself, loyalties were divided and many regarded the restoration as inevitable. Napoleon now had only about 75,000 troops to oppose his numerous adversaries, and these were little more than exhausted conscripts.

Still convinced that he could conclude favorable peace terms, Napoleon marched east with all speed and severely defeated an isolated Prussian corps at Rheims on 13 March. Blücher and Schwarzenberg promptly halted, but Napoleon's troops were too tired to engage them and instead went to the assistance of Macdonald, who had been pushed west to Provins. The Emperor again sought to threaten Schwarzenberg's rear on 17 March, but the Allied commander-in-chief withdrew once more, while on the same day Blücher defeated Marmont at Fismes. Finding the Allies refusing to answer his calls to reopen peace talks, Napoleon planned to march across

The defense of Clichy Gate, Paris. Napoleon left the defense of Paris to his incompetent brother, Joseph, who not only failed to arrest those pro-Bourbon agitators busily sowing dissension, spreading disinformation and Allied propaganda, but also allowed himself to be duped into believing that weapons, funds, and manpower could not be found to mount an adequate defense. He also neglected to order the repair of the city walls or undertake construction of earthworks and ramparts. (Ann Ronan Picture Library)

the Allied rear by moving toward St Dizier and Joinville on the upper Marne, thereby blocking Allied reinforcements for both armies and opening links with French forces holding Metz and Verdun.

Napoleon's only hope of survival lay in defeating his enemies in turn. He therefore planned to assault the garrison at Arcis-sur-Aube under Wrede. Displaying unusual energy, Schwarzenberg foiled this plan on 20 March by moving to Wrede's aid, and after two days' fighting the French were lucky to extricate themselves with only 3,000 casualties. Continuing his advance on the Marne, Napoleon reached St Dizier on 23 March, having first seen off a force of 8,000 cavalry dispatched to obstruct him.

Emboldened by news of Augereau's abandonment of Lyons, the Allies, meeting for a summit at Sommagices on 24 March, decided on a daring step. Winzingerode, with 10,000 men, would create a diversion by marching toward St Dizier, while the two main Allied armies would push directly on the capital, encouraged by the contents of an intercepted report written by the minister of police and intended for the Emperor:

The treasury, arsenals, and powder stores are empty. We have no resources left. The population is discouraged and discontented. It wants peace at any price. Enemies of the imperial government are sustaining and fomenting popular agitation. Still latent, it will become impossible to suppress unless the Emperor succeeds in keeping the Allies away from Paris.

On 25 March Schwarzenberg, en route for Paris, overran positions held by Mortier and Marmont at La-Fère-Champenoise. After waiting four days for reinforcements at St Dizier, Napoleon managed to repulse Winzingerode's advance on 26 March, but on learning of the defeat at La-Fère-Champenoise

he realized that he had failed to halt the Allied offensive. On the advice of senior generals, he therefore abandoned his plans to carry on the campaign on the frontiers and moved toward Paris on 28 March. On the same day, only 25 miles (40 km) from the capital, Schwarzenberg and Blücher combined forces at Meaux.

On 29 March Marie-Louise and the three-year-old king of Rome left Paris, and by the end of the following day so too had Joseph and the remaining government officials. At the same time Napoleon left the army at Troyes and rode rapidly for Paris, whose gates the Allies were now approaching. He was too late: that night French troops on Montmartre surrendered. Despite the presence of nearly 150,000 Allied troops in the capital, Napoleon initially refused to accept defeat. Proceeding south to Fontainebleau, he prepared to resume fighting, only to find his marshals refusing to carry on. Following a parade review on the afternoon of 3 April, Ney, Lefebvre and Moncey angrily interrupted the Emperor and Berthier to declare the futility of continued resistance. Napoleon explained his intention of driving on Paris, to which plan those assembled, now including Macdonald and Oudinot, offered a cold silence. 'We do not intend to expose Paris to

The battle of Montmartre, 30–31 March 1814. During this, the final action of the campaign before Napoleon's first abdication, Marshals Mortier and Marmont could muster fewer than 25,000 dispirited regulars and National Guards for the defense of Paris. Troops on the heights of Montmartre and Romainville offered some resistance, but with 150,000 Allies converging on the capital and Napoleon too far east to be of assistance, Marmont signed an armistice before dawn on the 31st. (AKG, Berlin)

the fate of Moscow,' Macdonald then declared. The Emperor remained steadfast, so prompting Ney to exclaim defiantly, 'The army will not march on Paris.' 'The Army will obey me,' Napoleon angrily replied, only to be disarmed by Ney's coup de grace: 'Sire: The army will obey its generals.' This, and word that Marmont had defected, prompted Napoleon to offer a conditional abdication on 4 April, followed two days later, upon its rejection, by an unconditional abdication. By the Treaty of Fontainebleau concluded 10 days later, Napoleon was granted a residence on the tiny Mediterranean island of Elba, and on 28 April he was conveyed there by a British warship. In Paris, Louis XVIII was restored to the throne and signed the Treaty of Paris on 30 April, bringing a formal end to the war and restoring the borders of his country to their 1792 limits.

Captain Cavalié Mercer, Royal Horse Artillery

Cavalié Mercer was born in 1783, the second son of General Mercer of the Royal Engineers, who had served in the War of American Independence on the staff of General Henry Clinton, and afterwards spent the next two decades as commanding engineer in the west of England. The younger Mercer attended the Military Academy at Woolwich, was commissioned into the Royal Artillery as a second lieutenant at the age of 16, and was posted to Ireland during the rebellion of 1798. He became a captain in December 1806 and in the following year was dispatched to South America with the expeditionary force under General Whitelocke (1757–1833), which suffered ignominious defeat. To his great personal regret Mercer did not see service in the Peninsular War, but was sent abroad during the Waterloo campaign while still a captain, in which capacity he commanded G Troop, Royal Horse Artillery.

Mercer, who related his experiences in his *Journal of the Waterloo Campaign*, was a candid, colorful and accurate observer of the events around him, and unlike many diarists before and since, fully acknowledged the fact that most soldiers have a limited view of the battlefield and seldom know anything of events occurring even a few hundred yards away.

Depend on it, he who pretends to give a general account of a great battle from his own observation deceives you – believe him not. He can see no farther (that is, if he be personally engaged in it) than the length of his nose; and how is he to tell what is passing two or three miles off, with hills and trees and buildings intervening, and all enveloped in smoke?

On the morning of Waterloo (18 June 1815) Mercer's troop was camped in an orchard, where his men busied themselves filling their canteens with rum, preparing oatmeal, cooking soup and digging up potatoes. When firing began he noticed that the bivouacs on the hillside suddenly became deserted, and as the firing grew louder he ordered the troop to be readied for maneuver. The kettles of soup were overturned and the troop was ready to move, but Mercer was entirely without orders.

It appeared to me we had been forgotten. All except only ourselves, were evidently engaged; and laboring under this delusion, I thought we had better get into the affair at once.

Reaching the field of battle, Mercer surveyed attractive open country, covered in fields of corn and dotted with thickets and woods. It was a relatively quiet position, left of the heavily fortified farm of Hougoumont. But as the battle intensified he watched as French cavalry and artillery became more active and round shot began to fall on his position. He briefly exchanged fire with a French battery, in the course of which one of his gunners was struck by a cannon shot:

I shall never forget the scream the poor lad gave when struck. It was one of the last they fired, and shattered his left arm to pieces as he stood between the waggons. That scream went to my very soul, for I accused myself of having caused his misfortune. I was, however, obliged to conceal my emotion from the men, who had turned to look at him; so, bidding them 'stand to their front', I continued my walk up and down, whilst Hitchins [the troop surgeon] ran to his assistance.

Round shot continued to plow into the soft mud around him, one striking a horse from the gun team, depriving it of the whole of its face below the eyes. Yet the beast remained alive and standing, leaving Mercer to order the farrier to end his misery, which he performed with a thrust through the heart with his saber. Shortly thereafter a senior officer, his face blackened from smoke, his sleeve torn open from French fire, galloped up, calling out, 'Left limber up, and as fast as you can.' In moments Mercer's troop was trundling toward the main ridge between Hougoumount and the Charleroi ridge, where the French were massing a large body of heavy cavalry in preparation for a charge.

Wellington's orders, the officer informed Mercer in clear terms, were explicit: if the cavalry were certain to reach the guns, Mercer and his men were to fire for as long as possible before retiring into the safety of the adjacent squares of infantry. As Mercer's troop ascended the reverse slope of the main Anglo–Allied position, the full spectacle and sound of battle burst upon him.

We breathed a new atmosphere, ... the air was suffocatingly hot, resembling that issuing from an oven. We were enveloped in thick smoke, and, malgré the incessant roar of cannon and musketry, could distinctly hear around us a mysterious humming noise, like that which one hears of a summer's evening proceeding from myriads of black beetles; cannon-shot, too, ploughed the ground in all directions, and so thick was the hail of balls and bullets that it seemed dangerous to extend the arm lest it should be torn off.

Hitchins, unaccustomed to such a cacophony, watched and listened with utter astonishment, twisting and turning in his saddle, declaring, 'My God, Mercer, what *is* that? What *is* all this noise? How curious! – how very curious!' When a cannon shot came hissing past, Mercer ordered him to withdraw, for the troop would need its surgeon intact.

Still, the troop reached the summit without loss, and the guns were unlimbered between two squares of Brunswick infantry to await the expected onslaught. No sooner had the first of Mercer's guns been maneuvered into position in the interval between the squares than he

perceived through the smoke the leading squadron of the advancing column coming on at a brisk trot. He immediately issued the order 'case shot!' and the guns unlimbered and were ready for action in moments. 'The very first round,' Mercer observed, '... brought down several men and horses. They continued, however, to advance.'

Meanwhile the Brunswickers had begun to issue musket fire, but as the square appeared unsteady he knew that he must remain with the guns and repulse the attackers or watch the infantry dissolve in panic. In this he knew that he must disobey Wellington's explicit order, and face the consequences later,

... a resolve that was strengthened by the effect of the remaining guns as they rapidly succeeded in coming to action, making terrible slaughter, and in an instant covering the ground with men and horses.

The horsemen nevertheless persevered, and though their progress was slowed to a walk they carried on, leading Mercer to the unpleasant conclusion that they would ride over him, though 'the carnage was frightful.'

In a hurried effort to retreat, the cavalry jostled and pushed through the debris, becoming:

a complete mob, into which we kept a steady fire of case-shot from our six pieces. The effect is hardly conceivable, and to paint this scene of slaughter and confusion impossible. Every discharge was followed by the fall of numbers, whilst the survivors struggled with each other, and I actually saw them using the pommels of their swords to fight their way out of the mêlée. Some, rendered desperate at finding themselves thus pent up at the muzzles of our guns, as it were, and others carried away by their horses, maddened with wounds, dashed through our intervals – few thinking of using their swords, but pushing furiously onward, intent only on saving themselves. At last the rear of the column, wheeling about, opened a passage, and the whole swept away at a much more rapid pace than they had advanced ... We then ceased firing; but as

French cuirassiers charging Highlanders deployed in
square. Hoping to clear the slopes in front of Mont St
Jean of its beleaguered defenders, Marshal Ney ordered
forward Milhaud's heavy cavalry corps, consisting of two
divisions of cuirassiers, which when joined by light cavalry
of the Imperial Guard, soon totaled 5,000 horsemen.
Wave upon wave of cavalry took temporary possession
of the guns but failed to spike them or to break any of
the British squares. Ney's failure to destroy the squares
with artillery fire, and the squandering of this splendid
cavalry, did much to hasten French defeat. (Roger-Viollet)

*they were still not far off, for we saw the tops of
their caps, having reloaded, we stood ready to
receive them should they renew the attack.*

One of the first men of Mercer's troop to
fall was a gunner named Butterworth,
responsible for sponging one of the guns.
Having just finished ramming down a shot,
he was in the process of stepping back away
from the mouth of the cannon when his foot
became stuck in the mud, thus pulling him
forward just as the gun was fired.

*As a man naturally does when falling, he threw
out both his arms before him, and they were blown
off at the elbows. He raised himself a little on his
two stumps, and looked up most piteously in my
face. To assist him was impossible – the safety of
all, everything, depended upon not slackening our
fire, and I was obliged to turn from him.*

Eventually Butterworth brought himself to
the rear but was discovered dead by the
roadside the following day, having bled to
death on the way to Waterloo while in search
of medical attention.

Meanwhile, the French launched a second
determined charge:

*None of your furious galloping charges was
this, but a deliberate advance, at a deliberate
pace, as of men resolved to carry their point.
They moved in profound silence, and the only
sound that could be heard from them amidst the
incessant roar of battle was the low thunder-like
reverberation of the ground beneath the
simultaneous tread of so many horses. On our
part was equal determination. Every man stood
steadily at his post, the guns ready, loaded with*

*a round-shot first and a case over it; the tubes
were in the vents; the port-fires glared and
sputtered behind the wheels; and my word alone
was wanting to hurl destruction on that goodly
show of gallant men and noble horses …*

*I … allowed them to advance unmolested until
the head of the column might have been about fifty
or sixty yards from us, and then gave the word,
'Fire!' The effect was terrible. Nearly the whole
leading rank fell at once; and the round-shot,
penetrating the column, carried confusion
throughout its extent. The ground, already
encumbered with victims of the first struggle,
became now almost impassable. Still, however,
these devoted warriors struggled on, intent only on
reaching us. The thing was impossible …*

*The discharge of every gun was followed by a
fall of men and horses like that of grass before
the mower's scythe … until gradually they
disappeared over the brow of the hill. We ceased
firing, glad to take breath.*

Mercer, on seeing yet a third attack on its way, cried: 'There they are again!' But it was a pathetic, or perhaps more appropriately, tragic display.

This time, it was child's play. They could not even approach us in any decent order, and we fired most deliberately; it was folly having attempted the thing. I was sitting on my horse near the right of my battery as they turned and began to retire once more. Intoxicated with success, I was singing out, 'Beautiful! – Beautiful!'

G Troop suffered 18 casualties at Waterloo, three of whom were killed in the battle, two others missing and presumed killed and the rest wounded, among them gunner Philip Hunt, whose left arm was shattered by a round shot. Mercer's troop lost 69 horses, nearly three times as many as

any other troop, and had expended an extraordinary amount of ammunition – about 700 rounds.

After the Napoleonic Wars Mercer was placed on half-pay until 1824, when he briefly served in Canada as a brevet major. In 1837, having attained the rank of lieutenant-colonel, he was again ordered to Canada, where he commanded the artillery in Nova Scotia during the border dispute which nearly led to war between the United States and Britain. He became a colonel in 1846 and major-general in 1854. Afterwards he was commander of the Dover garrison and retired from active service, though continued as colonel-commandant of the 9th Brigade of Royal Artillery. He spent the remainder of his life at his cottage outside Exeter and died in 1868 at the age of 85, immensely proud of having been present at the century's most decisive battle.

London: splendor and squalor

At the end of the Napoleonic Wars, London was Europe's largest and wealthiest city, with a population slightly exceeding a million. Notwithstanding acute poverty prevalent in some pockets of the metropolis, Londoners lived better than not only their rural countrymen but also those of any other city in the world. London was a city of artisans and business people, not an industrial center, and two decades of war had brought unparalleled prosperity, especially for the shipwrights in the lower Thames. Nevertheless, as the war began to reach its closing stages, not least the naval side of the conflict, which had slowed dramatically after Trafalgar, the demand for labor gradually fell and wages naturally followed suit.

London could be viewed as a city divided in socio-economic terms roughly according to the old divisions between east and west. Foreigners as well as Londoners themselves immediately recognized this reality. A French visitor, Louis Simond, wrote of 'a line of demarcation' passing through Soho Square which delineated rich and poor:

Every minute of longitude east is equal to as many degrees of gentility minus, or towards west, plus. This meridian line north and south, like that indicated by the compass, inclines west towards the north, and east towards the south, two or three points in such a manner as to place a certain part of Westminster on the side of fashion.

This division, and the constant stream of traffic moving between these distinctly different sections of the city, was noted by many contemporaries. 'The crowd, the carriages, and the mud increase rapidly as you advance from west to east,' Simond observed. He was particularly struck by the enormous size of the draft horses, but in some places one could also see bullocks, as

well. But the East End was not merely the site of poverty – it was the site of the City, where the 39 Incorporated Companies of Traders and Artisans, including the Merchant Taylors' Hall, the Ironmongers' Hall and many others were located. Here wealth was in the hands of bankers, stockbrokers, commission agents, and others whose new wealth resulted from growing investment in shipping, commerce and industrialization, all stimulated by a war that was now 20 years old.

While today we may admire the long rows of Georgian and Regency buildings still to be found in the West End, for many foreigners their first impressions proved disappointing. Simond found that:

London does not strike with admiration; it is regular, clean, convenient (I am speaking of the best part) but the site is flat; the plan monotonous; the predominant color of objects dingy and poor. It is altogether without great faults and without great beauties.

A Danish visitor named Feldborg thought the British capital compared poorly with his own, complaining of 'the gloomy solemnity' of the houses and the tiresome 'sameness of colossal piles of brick and mortar.' Richard Rush, the newly arrived American minister, was equally unimpressed: 'I am quite disappointed in the general exterior of the dwelling-houses,' he wrote, 'I had anticipated something better.' Part of this somber, arsenal-like appearance may be attributed to the Building Act of 1774, which restricted house construction to four standard types, and in so doing practically eradicated cosmetic ornamentation, placed restrictions on the length of projection on bayed shop-front windows, and obliged builders to confine window joinery to recesses in the wall. The effect was, for some contemporary observers anyway, a dreary regularity.

Nevertheless, visitors were impressed by the comforts of, at least, the homes of the well-to-do and middle classes. Whereas in Paris and other continental capitals most people lived in apartments, residents of London lived in houses, albeit narrow ones, which immediately opened into a private foyer with a staircase leading up two or three flights, in contrast to those in Paris where, as Simond pointed out, there were clear disadvantages: 'Instead of the abominable filth of the common entrance and common stairs of a French house, here you step from the very street on [to] a neat floor-carpet, the wall paneled or papered, a lamp in its glass bell hanging from the ceiling, and every apartment in the same style.'

Fog, or more properly 'smog', was ubiquitous in the capital, where by this time most residents and tradesmen had replaced open fires with coal-burning closed kitchen stoves to heat their homes and businesses, and to prepare meals. Domestic smoke emissions, combined with the output of the new factories of industrialization, produced an impenetrable smog which put tons of soot into the air and created a phenomenon that was to persist as a feature of London life well into the 20th century. Thus, especially in the mornings, heavy yellowish clouds would often envelop the streets, particularly so in the winter months, causing headaches, difficulty in breathing and, according to the accomplished contemporary physician Sir Frederick Treves, accounted for thousands of lives every year. Above the city, the resulting pollution would sometimes blacken the sky, while on the ground this 'pea soup' fog could grow thick enough to restrict normal vision to a matter of mere yards. Simond noted that in the winter 'smoke increases the general dingy hue, and terminates the length of every street with a fixed and grey mist, receding as you advance.' Indeed, January 1814 witnessed the worst fog in 60 years and nearly brought traffic to a standstill. Carriage accidents increased, with some vehicles overturning, and anyone who dared to proceed in a hackney coach could only do so at a walk, with a man on foot gingerly leading the horses, lantern in hand, calling out in an attempt to avoid collisions.

Fog on this magnitude paralyzed business and ordinary leisure, and one visitor noted that shops in Bond Street had their lamps lit at noon. Some, like J. P. Malcolm, observed with surprise when one early morning he could make out the end of his street:

Then lengthened the perspective, and enabled the eye to penetrate depths unfathomable at eight o'clock, and showed retiring houses at distances I had never seen them before. The fanciful decorations of shop windows, doors, and the fresh-painted fronts, had each their relief; and the brazen appearance of the gilt names [that] had vanished with the smoke, now darted with due lustre.

Princess Lieven described it as giving 'a vivid picture of chaos and the void. There is something positively hellish in the effect exerted by the sight of that opaque atmosphere.'

In addition to air pollution, the Thames was the natural repository for rubbish and human waste, while horse and livestock traffic left the streets dotted with droppings, the avoidance of which required a degree of wariness on the part of pedestrians wishing to cross a road. There was more to avoid than this: those on foot crossed thoroughfares, with no controls on coach and wagon traffic, at their peril. The resulting smell of a crowded city without a modern sewage system can scarcely be imagined. Many streets were unpaved; when dry they produced clouds of dust and when wet they turned to mud. Apart from the fog, the smell, and the mess, there was also a considerable amount of noise, as street peddlers and hawkers called out to passers-by as horse-drawn vehicles of various descriptions trundled along. As the age of compulsory education was two generations in the future, many of those working and playing in the streets were children.

Indeed, in the absence of child labor laws, minors could be employed for more than 12 hours a day, sometimes in dangerous conditions. In March 1813, for instance, Thomas Pitt, aged eight, working as an apprentice chimney sweep, or 'climbing boy', was instructed to descend the chimney of a 'brewhouse' in Upper Thames Street, where he became trapped. A Parliamentary inquiry learned that the boy's boss:

... had no sooner extinguished the fire than he suffered the lad to go down; and the consequence, as might be expected, was his almost immediate death, in a state, no doubt, of inexpressible agony ... Soon after his descent, the master, who remained at the top, was apprehensive that something had happened, and therefore desired him to come up; the answer of the boy was, 'I cannot come up, master, I must die here.'

Despite the efforts of a bricklayer to break into the chimney, the boy died, having become trapped against a red hot iron pipe inside the flue.

Contemporaries generally divided London into 'Town', meaning the West End, and 'the City'. Modern-day Kensington, Chelsea and Knightsbridge were nothing more than tiny country villages with open country extending from every side. Places like Hampstead were yet to be built on, while, on the south bank of the river, Clapham and Camberwell, the first commuter suburbs, were only just beginning to develop. Considering today's urban sprawl, it is scarcely conceivable that from Whitehall and Westminster one could look across the Thames and see the hills of Surrey.

'The City' was the financial section, occupying part of the area once surrounded by the old medieval walls of London, with the Thames to the south, the Inns of Court and Temple Bar to the west, and the Tower to the east. This was a place of merchants and traders of all descriptions and the site of the Bank of England and the Royal Exchange. Few people apart from some of the merchants themselves actually lived here.

The West End then, as today, referred to the fashionable part of London, including Westminster, St James's Palace, and Buckingham Palace, the government buildings along Whitehall, including the Treasury, the Foreign Office, the headquarters of the army, known as Horse Guards, Westminster Abbey, and the Houses of Parliament. Mayfair was the prime situation for the aristocracy and upper classes, and was the site of famous men's clubs in Pall Mall and the fashionable shops of Bond Street. The western-most side of Mayfair was Park Lane, which overlooked Hyde Park, a semi-wild haven, theoretically open to the public, but in reality the preserve of the aristocracy and upper classes generally. Here the *noblesse* and social elite paraded around the Ring on horseback or in carriages, there to see and be seen. Captain Gronow described it thus:

The company which then congregated daily about five was composed of dandies and women in the best society; the men mounted on such horses as England alone could then produce ... Many of the ladies used to drive into the park in a carriage called a vis-à-vis, which held only two persons. The hammer-cloth, rich in heraldic designs, the powdered footman in smart liveries, and a coachman who assumed all the gaiety and appearance of a wigged archbishop, were indispensable. The equipages were generally much more gorgeous than at a later period, when democracy invaded the parks, and introduced ... shabby-genteel carriages and servants. The carriage company consisted of the most celebrated beauties; and in those earlier days you never saw any of the lower or middle classes of London intruding themselves in regions which, with a sort of tacit understanding, were given up exclusively to persons of rank and fashion.

London was a city of contrasts. Generally speaking, the further east one traveled, the poorer housing conditions became. Unlike today, the docks of the East End were crowded with shipping. Few people lived on the South Bank. There were pleasure gardens at Vauxhall, Lambeth was nothing more than

the site of the palace occupied by the
Archbishop of Canterbury, and Greenwich
was the home of the royal hospital for retired
seamen. There were of course no railways,
and fewer bridges spanning the Thames than
there are today. To cross the river one had to
pay a small fee, and there were considerably
fewer places to cross than there are today.
One could go via London Bridge – an old
stone extension opposite the City and just
west of the Tower – across Blackfriars Bridge
near the Temple, or, in the West End, across
Westminster Bridge, next to Parliament.
Waterloo and Southwark bridges were not
erected until a few years after the Napoleonic
Wars. One could of course cross or proceed
up or down the Thames by boat, secured by a
small fee to one of the many watermen who
plied the river for this purpose.

London offered everything imaginable in
the way of basic necessities, but also of
comfort and luxury: everything from bakers,
booksellers, stationers, fruiterers, china
shops, seal-makers, apothecaries,
candle-makers, drapers, confectioners, and
coffee houses. All foreign visitors agreed that
London was crammed with shops, perhaps

London, 1814. This print by Thomas Rowlandson, one of the
leading satirists of the Regency period, pokes fun at the
chaos of the capital's streets. Two coachmen, ferrying their
privileged passengers, strike one another in a frenzied
competition for passage, oblivious to the street peddlers
whose baskets they have upset and the other vehicles trying
to make headway in an age when traffic went virtually
unregulated. (Guildhall Library, Corporation of London)

confirming Napoleon's derogatory
description of Britain as 'a nation of
shopkeepers'. One foreigner remarked on
the 'opulence and splendour' of such
establishments. These were specifically
located in Mayfair and St James's, though
shopping might take the fashionable
consumer to Covent Garden, the Strand and
the City. The area around St James's catered
mainly to men, being the site of their clubs,
such as White's and Brooks's, bachelor
accommodation and exclusive shops,
specializing in men's clothing, hats,
umbrellas, canes, snuff boxes, and so on.
St James's Street itself was, socially speaking –
and whether riding in an open carriage or,
above all, on foot – off-limits to women who
wished to count themselves among the
refined and respectable, as men tended to sit

in the windows of their clubs to eye the passers-by.

Bond Street, however, was deemed appropriate for ladies, and there could be found a circulating library which offered a range of books, particularly novels including Gothic romances, those of Walter Scott, the most popular writer of this time and, of course, Jane Austen's novels. In the last years of the Napoleonic Wars she published *Sense and Sensibility* (1811), *Pride and Prejudice* (1813), *Mansfield Park* (1814), and *Emma* (1815), none of which made explicit reference to the conflict then raging on the Continent. Those admiring the latest portraits in progress or who desired to commission a likeness of themselves, could find the studios of Sir Thomas Lawrence and Hoppner in Bond Street. In an age before photography, this was a highly popular means of preserving oneself for future generations, and Lawrence was especially prized for his sometimes not so subtle 'improvements' to those sitters with a less than pleasing countenance. Whether such flattery was necessary or not, a portrait by Sir Thomas would cost his subjects the enormous sum of 700 guineas, and they would have to put their names on a waiting list for the privilege.

Fashionable young men were particularly drawn to 'Gentleman' Jackson's boxing saloon in Bond Street, as well as to the most expensive tailor in London, Weston, whose customers included no less than the Prince Regent, 'Beau' Brummell, and most of his ilk. Many such men lived in bachelor lodgings on the top floors of Bond Street businesses, converted for the purpose and nearly as exclusive as those in St James's or the new luxurious flats created by the conversion of the Duke of York's private residence in the Albany in 1802.

Those interested in prints – a very popular form of publication – and other expensive articles, naturally ventured to Ackermann's shop in the Strand, where the Savoy Hotel now stands. There one could find prints of all descriptions, but particularly of architecture, nature and political caricatures,

in which this period abounded. Among the men whose work Ackermann sold were Gillray, Rowlandson, and Cruickshank, but there were many others who poked fun at politicians, the Prince Regent, Napoleon, and the French in general, as well as the current fashion of visiting the countryside with its peculiar interest in lakes, forests, abandoned castles, and anything 'Gothic'. Sometimes prints appeared as parts of books with satirical text or verse, but in whatever form they assumed they were a fundamental part of fashionable culture at this time. Ackermann's 'Repository of Arts' also sold a wide range of other goods, such as decorative screens, card racks, and flower stands.

Simply being seen in public, whether in one's carriage, or strolling through Mayfair, became a mainstay of daily life among the upper classes. In the course of this promenade one was certain to meet one's friends and show off new clothes and accessories. After a tiring day shopping people could stop at Gunter's, a confectionery in Berkeley Square, or at Friburg and Treyer in the Haymarket to sample and buy snuff imported from parts far afield.

In short, London was a cornucopia of every imaginable object, from the cheap to the extravagant. For those blessed with sufficient funds and time, shopping became an end in itself, what we might today call 'conspicuous consumption'. Those with disposable incomes could buy clothes of velvet, lined with satin, muslin handkerchiefs, gloves, boots, silk shirts, furs, fancy waistcoats, embroidered dressing gowns, breeches made of doe hide, and add to these buttons of silk, ivory, silver, gold, or jewels.

Sartorial splendor, in fact, abounded during this time – epitomized by the Prince Regent – and there was no end to the cost that the determined shopper could incur in acquiring an impressive wardrobe. Specialist craftsmen ensured that every need was provided: button-makers, or those who sold only whips, or spurs, or swords. Some shops made only drapery, caps, hats, gloves, or hosiery. There were leather-makers who made boots, saddles, sabretaches, and horse equipment, and *plumassiers* who, from exotic birds such as egrets, birds of paradise, and peacocks, to the less extravagant but by no means inexpensive ostrich, provided the feathers which were such an essential fashion accessory, especially for court appearances. Scent and cosmetics during this time were luxuries, and perfumiers and purveyors of powder, paste, and pomatum sold items to both sexes. There were scented oils of roses, jasmine, orange, and many other forms to attract, and to cover bad odor, whether derived from the body or the street. Like today, the eager consumer could part with cash very quickly at the jewelers, the most fashionable of which were Hamlet's, whose patrons included many members of the British and foreign royalty, Thomas Gray of Sackville Street and Phillips of Bond Street. There was also the best-known goldsmith and jewelers, Rundell and Bridge, on Ludgate Hill, the Prince Regent's favorite.

Evidence of the prosperity of London – and the nation at large – was demonstrated to Richard Rush, the newly arrived American minister, when he looked round the City shortly after the end of the war:

Went through Temple Bar into the city, in contradistinction to the West-end of London, always called town … If I looked with any wonder on the throngs at the West-end, more cause is there for it here. The shops stand, side by side, for entire miles. The accumulation of things is amazing. It would seem impossible that there can be purchasers for them all, until you consider what multitudes there are to buy; then, you are disposed to ask how the buyers can be supplied. In the middle of the streets, coal-waggons and others as large, carts, trucks, vehicles of every sort, loaded in every way, are passing. They are in two close lines, reaching further than the eye can see, going reverse ways. The horses come so near to the foot pavement, which is crowded with people, that their hoofs, and the great wheels of the waggons, are only a few inches from them. In this manner the whole procession is in movement, with all its complicated noise. It confounds the senses to be

among it all. You would anticipate constant accidents; yet they seldom happen … The Custom House, and black forest of ships below London Bridge, I saw by a glimpse: that was enough to show that the Thames was choked up with vessels and boats of every description, much after the manner that I beheld Cheapside and Fleet Street to be choked with vehicles that move on land …

While London, then as now, had its fair share of attractive features, walking its streets required vigilance. Crossing a road amidst the tumult of horse-drawn traffic – from phaetons, carriages and coaches to wagons and carts – could result in serious injury or death to the unwary. Those actually in traffic had then – as now – to contend with jams and accidents, at a time when there was no traffic management by lines on the roads, signs, or lights. London had a rush hour, particularly acute in the City, and those who tried to travel the Strand and Fleet Street between noon and five found themselves facing roads choked with vehicles of sundry descriptions, from beautiful open carriages like the tilbury, to the barouche, hackney coach, phaeton, and curricle, pulled by between two and six horses. This was, moreover, still a time when, on certain days of the week, the streets of the City became thronged with oxen being driven to market. On the Thames, major vessels could not proceed up the river past London Bridge, and directions for navigation often referred to being 'above bridge' or 'below bridge'. The bulk of traffic originated at 'the Docks' where companies such as the East India Company had built vast stretches of wharves in the late eighteenth century.

Of the people themselves, Simond observed that 'I have heard no cries in the streets, and seen few beggars.' He does not appear to have ventured into the truly destitute sections of the city, but he shared the view of most foreigners that the working classes dressed reasonably well and looked strong and healthy. Poverty was certainly present in London, but it was not obvious to the visitor, being restricted largely to the run-down courts and alleys circling the City, but also scattered in places where unskilled laborers from Ireland could find a place to eke out a miserable existence, such as in the rookeries between St Martin's Lane and Bedford Street, where violence was commonplace, or in Thieving Lane and the Sanctuaries of Westminster. These places, and Petty France, off St James's Park and near Parliament, were off-limits to anyone who looked as if he had something worth stealing. One French princess found, after emerging from an opera in the Haymarket one evening, that passage through the area between the theater and St James's Market was a rather unsavory experience.

Crime was a serious problem and driving and walking alone across a seemingly empty heath or taking an unfamiliar path could prove harrowing at best and fatal at worst. In January 1814 robbers held up the Buckingham stage-coach in Oxford Street in the middle of the day. Newspapers reported the Strand thronging with men intent on theft and daylight robbery. An entire criminal gang went on trial in February, while in the spring a number of victims were held up at gun point and obliged to hand over their valuables. Pubs were not always safe. Robbers struck during business hours to take cash and watches from the proprietor as well as from his patrons. Such crimes are hardly surprising under the circumstances, for London had no police force. There were watch houses at intervals throughout the city, where, as one contemporary guide pointed out: 'a parochial constable attends in rotation, to see that order prevails, to receive offenders, and deliver them the next morning to the sitting Magistrate.' The same publication advised that those finding themselves accosted should cry out repeatedly 'Watch!' with the expectation that several such men would come instantly to their aid, but the fact remained that these were simply a handful of unarmed, old men – hardly a source of comfort or protection to helpless citizens with pistols to their heads. Indeed, Robert Southey, the noted historian and poet, observed that their main function

was 'to inform the good people of London every half an hour of the state of the weather'. They were in fact worse than useless to him, for in calling out the time throughout the course of the night, poor Southey was deprived of sleep.

Punishments reflected the harshness of the times. It was, after all, not long since the 18th-century reforms had brought to an end the practice of displaying the heads of the executed on spikes at Temple Bar. Rampant crime stood side by side with draconian punishments. Men like Sir Samuel Romilly, and the celebrated prison reformer Elizabeth Fry, had spent many years arguing for reform of the judicial process in an attempt to reduce the number of capital offenses, to shorten lengthy prison sentences and to render the punishment more consistent with the gravity of the crime. 'The ancient criminal code of England,' Romilly announced, 'is the most sanguinary in existence.' Proof of this was the fact that in April 1814 Parliament renewed its debate on the propriety of disemboweling convicted traitors and decapitation after hanging. It is a fascinating barometer of contemporary attitudes toward criminal justice that MPs did not reach a definitive conclusion to these issues. Times were harsh and punishments reflected this: in January 1814 a soldier was hanged at Execution Dock for the murder of an officer, while during the same month another soldier, Thomas Beckworth, was sentenced to receive 550 lashes for deserting his regiment and self-mutilation. Such punishments sometimes amounted to a death sentence and in Beckworth's case he probably survived because of the intervention of a doctor, who recognized that the offender could not survive any further punishment.

Civil executions were held in public and throngs of people normally attended these grisly events. In March 1814 an unscrupulous doctor by the name of Buckley was hanged for the accidental death of his pregnant mistress, Dolly Rosthorp, which resulted from a botched abortion. In April seven men mounted the scaffold erected in front of Debtors' Doors at Newgate Prison, while in May 23-year-old William Botteril was hanged in front of spectators for forging a bill of exchange. Such spectacles were more than a means of deterring crime: however much the fact was condemned by increasing numbers of progressive individuals, public executions constituted a form of entertainment, and they drew crowds like few other events.

People found a more pleasant reason for gathering in 1814, however, for the first few months of the year were the coldest on record since the Great Freeze of 1739–40. In February the Thames froze over – a phenomenon never since repeated – and was soon converted by enterprising Londoners into a fair, in which the watermen posted signs directing people from the north bank to patronize the hundreds of booths erected on the ice, festooned with streamers and flags. Thousands thronged down the thoroughfare nicknamed 'Freezeland Street' which ran between the booths that lined the banks to buy gingerbread, pies, oysters, gin and beer, toys, books, satirical prints, and silly rhyming ballads, and to play carnival games along this makeshift avenue stretching from London Bridge to Southwark.

In general, wealthy Londoners of this time spent considerably more time outside than they do today, indulging in picnics that lasted all day, boat parties on the Thames, or excursions to Kew Gardens, or rides in Richmond Park. For those not inclined to venture this far, London was nothing like as built-up as today, and contained an abundance of quiet green spaces and gardens quite apart from Green Park and St James's Park, though many of these places charged a nominal admission of a penny or two. One could enjoy cakes and pastries at the 'tea garden' where King's Cross Station now stands, or at Pancras Wells or the now long-since disappeared Marylebone Gardens, which gave way to houses in what is now Cavendish Square and Portman Place, a decade after the war ended. There were buns and ginger beer at Regent's Park, while at Islington Spa one could indulge in drinking the waters of the spring there, thought to impart beneficial medicinal effects, though again construction was beginning to encroach on its gardens before the war was over.

The gardens at Vauxhall, with their numerous fêtes, masquerades, concerts, and other forms of entertainment, were the city's greatest outdoor attraction. Admission was two shillings – a price that naturally limited the clientele. The gardens were partly enclosed by high walls, lined with groves of trees and gravel walks, with mazes, quiet nooks and secluded areas. Some parts were carefully manicured while others were left largely wild, and offered views of the river. There were specially designed caves and grottos and waterfalls, with marble statues at various points consistent with neo-classical contemporary tastes. Handel's music was frequently played at the concert hall there. Pleasure seekers could admire the work at the picture gallery, dance in the hall, and buy refreshments from the booths while watching a balloon ascent, jugglers, acrobats, and tightrope walkers. At night the gardens were dramatically illuminated with thousands of lanterns, colored lamps and chandeliers hidden in the trees, while magnificent firework displays were staged over the river. The Prince Regent and his set often reserved the gardens at Vauxhall for elaborate parties and festive occasions, though the fête given by the prince in celebration of the victory at Vitoria in 1813 proved disastrous, with thousands turning up with tickets to a venue which the organizers optimistically imagined could accommodate everyone.

Viscount Castlereagh, British Foreign Secretary

Robert Stewart, Viscount Castlereagh (1769–1822), was probably Britain's greatest foreign secretary. Born in Ulster in 1760 to an Anglo–Irish family, he went to Cambridge and entered Parliament in 1790, where he became a close adherent of Pitt and supported the Union of Ireland with the rest of Great Britain. In 1804 he became Secretary of State for War and the Colonies, in which capacity he planned the expedition to Portugal commanded by Sir Arthur Wellesley, later Duke of Wellington, but left office in 1809 as a political scapegoat for the failed Walcheren expedition to Holland. He is best known for his tenure as foreign secretary under the Liverpool government between 1812 and 1822, during which time he was pivotal not only in raising the Sixth Coalition against France, but in planning and implementing the political reconstruction of Europe after Napoleon's fall. The origins of the general European settlement of 1815 may be found in the Treaty of Chaumont, an innovative agreement principally the work of Castlereagh's deft diplomacy, and the subject of this brief review of the Foreign Secretary's varied accomplishments.

Castlereagh, together with the Austrian Foreign Minister, Prince Metternich, played a leading role not only in developing a practical solution to the political upheaval wrought by more than two decades of war, but also in balancing the relative strengths of the Great Powers. He established a system of international cooperation which helped preserve peace on the Continent for several decades after 1815. Castlereagh was regarded as aloof, bordering on the arrogant, being described by one contemporary as 'impenetrably cold'. Unlike his distinguished contemporaries, Pitt, Canning, and Fox, Castlereagh was no skillful public speaker, yet in the realm of foreign affairs he understood the importance of maintaining the balance of power on the Continent, and in upholding British supremacy at sea and in the colonial world.

While seeking to preserve the Sixth Coalition, Castlereagh recognized that while his country could not offer troops for the

Viscount Castlereagh, British Foreign Secretary, 1812–22. A skilled negotiator with a firm grasp of power politics, Castlereagh managed his country's foreign policy during the crucial years 1813–15 through his personal presence at Allied headquarters as well as at the Congress of Vienna which followed the peace. In close collaboration with his Austrian colleague, Prince Metternich, Castlereagh established a new political order in Europe that preserved peace for the next 40 years. (Philip Haythornthwaite)

main theater of operations in Germany, Britain was already playing a vital role in the struggle against Napoleon. While the Treasury supplied tens of millions of pounds in subsidies to Spain, Portugal, Russia, Prussia, and other states, Wellington had close to 100,000 British, Portuguese and Spanish troops operating in northern Spain. The Royal Navy, moreover, had long since kept French ports under close blockade and had swept the seas of French maritime trade. All of these contributions to the struggle gave Castlereagh grounds for believing that Britain was entitled to a voice in continental affairs, and when he set out for Allied headquarters at the end of 1813 he did so with the confident expectation that Britain was not only the equal of the other major European powers, but that his country's status ought to be recognized in the treaty that was to bind them to a series of common objectives.

Nevertheless, defending British interests formed only part of his responsibilities, for Castlereagh would have to draw on considerable powers of discretion and conciliation in order to assuage the suspicions the Allied leaders harbored toward one another, and to ensure that the coalition survived long enough to defeat the common enemy. The precise terms to be offered to Napoleon remained as yet unsettled.

Castlereagh left for Allied headquarters on 20 December 1813, his principal objective being to represent Britain at the peace conference to be convened in the event that Napoleon accepted the Frankfurt proposals. As foreign secretary, negotiating in person, Castlereagh drafted his own instructions, based on Pitt's 1805 plan for the reconstruction of postwar Europe. Particular emphasis was laid on the importance of ensuring an independent Holland, with a secure border, including the strategically vital port of Antwerp. Castlereagh also recognized that an independent Belgium could not hope to defend itself and would probably have to be joined to Holland in order to form a more secure state against a resurgent France. Yet his plans did not call for the destruction of France as a major

power: future European security depended on a balance, and France naturally formed an essential element in this scheme as a counterweight to the pretensions of other possible contenders for continental supremacy, particularly Russia. He was therefore not convinced that France need necessarily be ruled by the Bourbon line: Napoleon and his successors could possibly remain in power.

Castlereagh was also prepared to offer the return of captured French and Dutch colonies in exchange for security on the Continent, but was unwilling to compromise over such strategically important possessions as Malta, Mauritius, and the Cape of Good Hope. Bringing peace to Europe and re-establishing political order was not enough. As he understood from his political mentor, Pitt, some mechanism had to exist to provide for future security. The novel means of maintaining the wartime coaliton after the conclusion of peace would ensure that France did not again threaten her neighbors. Maintaining good relations between the coalition partners was central to Castlereagh's policy, and as Britain had no territorial aspirations on mainland Europe, the Foreign Secretary was in a strong position to keep the Allied powers on good terms.

Castlereagh reached Basle on 18 January 1814, where he met most of the Allied sovereigns and ministers, including Metternich, with whom he struck up an instant friendship, establishing a rapport that would enable the two statesmen to play a decisive role in European diplomacy for the crucial remaining months of the war and in the period of reconstruction afterwards. Indeed, the negotiations of this period involved close contact with diplomats, statesmen, and sovereigns, and much of Castlereagh's success, notwithstanding his reputation among some of his contemporaries, may be attributed to his agreeable manner and charm. Wilhelm von Humboldt, the former Prussian foreign minister, said of him: 'He conducts himself with moderation and firmness, and from the first moment was a conciliating influence here.' The Tsar, too, respected Castlereagh, though Alexander and Castlereagh certainly had their differences, not least the Tsar's wish for Bernadotte to ascend the French throne.

There were other sensitive differences between the Allies, and the British position had to be made clear from the outset. In his first meeting with the Allied foreign ministers Castlereagh argued that future European security depended on the reduction of France to her 'ancient' frontiers:

To suppose that the Allies could rest satisfied with any arrangement substantially short of reducing France within her ancient limits, was to impute to them an abandonment of their most sacred duty, which, if made with a view to peace, must fail of its object, as the public mind of Europe would never remain tranquil under so improvident an arrangement.

When the Allied sovereigns left Switzerland and joined Schwarzenberg's headquarters in France, tensions obliged Castlereagh to play a mediating role between Alexander and Metternich, for the Tsar did not wish to negotiate with Napoleon, but instead to push on to Paris. Largely through Castlereagh's intervention the Allies agreed to extend terms to Napoleon while continuing to prosecute the campaign. In short, France would be offered her prewar frontiers of 1792. Metternich in fact would have conceded more, while Alexander wished to offer nothing at all. Castlereagh's compromise placated them all and preserved intact an alliance whose individual members often pursued conflicting aims, particularly over the issue of territorial compensation for themselves in the postwar settlement.

Castlereagh proved unable to pin down Alexander on the precise form of compensation he sought at war's end. The Foreign Secretary wanted the coalition to state its war aims clearly and comprehensively, so as to avoid disagreements between the various parties that might arise when peace was concluded

and the powers could sit down and redraw the map. Alexander, however, would not commit his aims to paper, though it was well known that he wished to expand into Poland, and this secrecy contributed to Castlereagh's growing closeness with Metternich. Castlereagh wanted 'a just equilibrium or balance of power in Europe,' and he argued that, in a congress to be held after the war, Prussia should receive compensation in Saxony both in return for the losses she had sustained in 1807, and for her participation in the present coalition. Castlereagh offered to assist Bernadotte in his bid for Norway (a possession of Napoleon's ally, Denmark). With regard to Alexander and the Polish question, Castlereagh would offer no firm opinion, reserving that important question to a future congress to be held after the war.

Terms were presented to Napoleon and negotiations for peace began at Châtillon on 5 February. In the meantime, Castlereagh worked hard to establish a formal alliance, binding the Allies by written agreement to a common object. By the Treaty of Chaumont, signed on 1 March, they agreed to prosecute the war until they had achieved the following aims: complete independence for Switzerland and Spain, the latter under the restored King Ferdinand IV; Italy was to be free of French control and the various states of that peninsula were to be restored to their respective legitimate rulers; there was to be an enlarged Holland, to include Belgium as a more secure frontier; Germany was to be reconstituted into a confederation, reducing the number of states and creating larger units in order to provide protection from future French attack. To fund the alliance, Britain would furnish £5 million in subsidies to be equally divided between Russia, Prussia, and Austria over the course of the ensuing year. In return these nations were each to maintain 150,000 men in the field until the conclusion of the war. Finally, no power could sign a separate peace with France without unanimous consent.

The Treaty of Chaumont was in fact revolutionary in diplomatic terms, for it

Prince Metternich, one of the greatest statesmen of the
19th century. As foreign minister he persuaded Francis to
bring Austria into the Sixth Coalition in 1813, at the
same time advocating a negotiated settlement with
Napoleon, including the possibility of his retaining the
throne. Metternich sought the establishment of a balance
of power on the Continent and recognized the necessity
of a stable, intact, and reasonably strong France as a
counterweight to the growing power of Russia and
Prussia. Together with Castlereagh, Metternich shares the
credit as the architect of the successful peace settlement
established after Waterloo. (AKG, Berlin)

established for the first time the principle of
peacetime collective defense by binding the
signatories to support one another with
troops (60,000 in each case) in the event of
attack, extending to a period of 20 years after
the conclusion of the war. Naturally it
contained elements common to great treaties
of the past. It laid down, for instance, the
principle that the Great Powers would,
among themselves, redraw the political map
of postwar Europe as they saw fit, leaving
lesser powers to discuss matters confined to
their immediate region, all, of course, subject
to the veto of the leading nations.

Chaumont was effectively Castlereagh's
personal achievement, and once Napoleon
made the fatal decision to reject the
proposals put to him in February 1814, the
unity Castlereagh had forged remained
unbroken, enabling the Allies, bound by a
mutually agreed set of objectives, to bring to
bear their combined power against a nation
that could not otherwise be beaten. Many
points were naturally reserved for discussion
later in the year, to be held at an
international conference to include all the
nations of Europe – great and small – but the
later success of the celebrated Congress of
Vienna may in great measure be attributed
to Castlereagh's achievements during the
war itself.

Dénouement at Waterloo

On 26 February 1815 Napoleon escaped from exile on the island of Elba, landed in the south of France and marched on Paris, gathering adherents and winning the loyalty of the army as he went. Two Allied forces in the Low Countries were of immediate concern: an Anglo–Dutch army of 90,000 men under the Duke of Wellington, and 120,000 Prussians under Marshal Blücher. Napoleon's plan was to strike at each in turn, thus preventing them from joining forces. On 15 June he crossed the river Sambre with his Army of the North of 125,000 men and moved through Charleroi on the Brussels road. His purpose was to separate the Allies and defeat them in turn. Two battles were fought on the following day, at Ligny and at Quatre Bras. At the former the Prussians were defeated with serious losses but managed to withdraw north to Wavre. A Prussian captain noted the dreadful condition of his men toward the end of the fighting:

The light of the long June day was beginning to fail … The men looked terribly worn out after the fighting. In the great heat, gunpowder smoke, sweat and mud had mixed into a thick crust of dirt, so that their faces looked almost like those of mulattos, and one could hardly distinguish the green collars and facings on their tunics. Everybody had discarded his stock [neck scarf]; grubby shirts or hairy brown chests stuck out from their open tunics; and many who had been unwilling to leave the ranks on account of a slight wound wore a bandage they had put on themselves. In a number of cases blood was soaking through.

As a result of the fighting in the villages for hours on end, and of frequently crawling through hedges, the men's tunics and trousers had got torn, so that they hung in rags and their bare skin showed through.

At Quatre Bras, Wellington, though forced to retire to protect Brussels, had not been crushed, with the result that though both Allied armies had been kept apart, they were capable of fighting another day. On 17 June Wellington marched north and deployed his tired army on a ridge just south of Mont St Jean. Having detached a corps to observe the Prussians at Wavre, 12 miles (19 km) west of Wellington's position, Napoleon established his army, now 72,000 strong, on a ridge just south of the Anglo–Allied position.

Wellington had 68,000 men, comprising mainly mixed Anglo–Hanoverian divisions, and some Dutch–Belgian divisions. Most of these he placed along a two-mile (3 km), crescent-shaped ridge, though 18,000 were detached 5 miles (8 km) west at Tubize, to prevent the French from making a wide sweep around to the west and from threatening his right flank. On Wellington's left stood the villages of Papelotte and La Haye. In his center stood the farm of La Haye Sainte near the crossroads formed by the Ohain and Charleroi–Brussels roads. On his right, and somewhat forward of his main line, lay the chateau of Hougoumont, which included woods, farm buildings, and a garden. Wellington recognized the tactical importance of Hougoumont and La Haye Sainte, and placed strong garrisons in each. These strong-points presented obstacles to a French attack on the Allied right and center, and could offer enfilading fire to any opposing troops that sought to bypass them. Hougoumont was large enough, moreover, to make a sweep round Wellington's right more difficult, though not impossible.

The battle began when, around 11.30 am, a large force of French infantry under Prince Jerome Bonaparte attacked Hougoumont, held by elements of the Foot Guards and a battalion of Nassauers. Fighting would, in fact, rage around Hougoumont all day, but all French attacks were repulsed. At one

point the French actually forced the gate, but the Guards managed to close it and avert disaster. Later, the chateau was set on fire by French howitzers, but with reinforcements the defenders managed to keep possession of the remaining buildings despite unrelenting assaults. While the fighting continued around Hougoumont, at about noon the French massed 80 guns against the British center in preparation for the attack of Lieutenant-General Drouet, Comte d'Erlon (1765–1844). The effect, only 600 yards (549 m) from the Allied line, was horrific, despite Wellington's deployment of his infantry on the reverse side of the slope.

At about 1.30 pm, d'Erlon's corps of four divisions ascended the slope, the troops stretching from Papelotte to La Haye Sainte in one great mass, much of it toward the position held by Lieutenant-General Sir Thomas Picton (1758–1815). Wellington's

Coldstream Guards closing the gate at Hougoumont, a fortified farm which became the focus of some of the bloodiest fighting at Waterloo. This vital strongpoint in the Allied line nearly fell when axe-wielding French infantry broke open the great north door, allowing a handful of men to enter the courtyard. Colonel Macdonnell, sword in hand, along with four other Coldstreamers, just managed to close the gate, an action which Wellington later claimed had been essential to success that day. (Trustees of the National Museum of Scotland)

artillery fired on the advancing columns, inflicting heavy casualties on the front ranks, and when the French reached the top of the ridge they met devastating close-range fire from the red-coated infantry, followed up with a bayonet charge led by Picton, who was shot and killed. At the same time, Lieutenant-General the Earl of Uxbridge (1768–1854), commander of the cavalry, ordered the two heavy brigades behind the Allied center to charge in order to capitalize

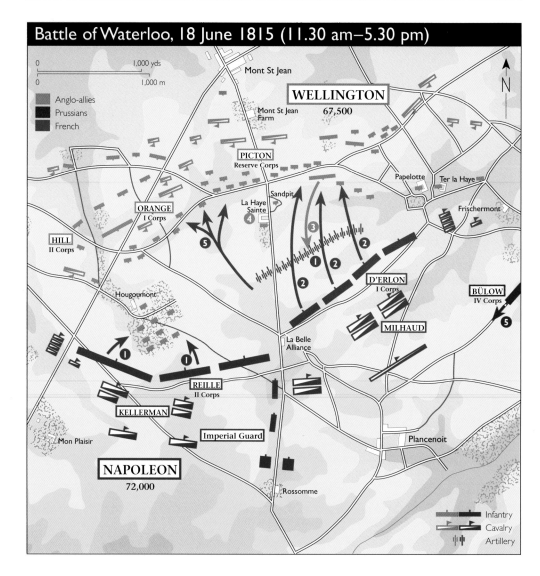

Battle of Waterloo, 18 June 1815 (11.30 am–5.30 pm)

0   1,000 yds
0   1,000 m

- Anglo-allies
- Prussians
- French

Mont St Jean

WELLINGTON   67,500

Mont St Jean Farm

PICTON
Reserve Corps

Papelotte   Ter la Haye

Sandpit

La Haye Sainte   **4**

Frischermont

ORANGE
I Corps

HILL
II Corps   **5**   **3**   **2**

1   **2**   **2**

Hougoumont   **2**   **D'ERLON**
I Corps   **BÜLOW**
IV Corps

MILHAUD   **5**

La Belle Alliance

REILLE
II Corps

KELLERMAN

Mon Plaisir   **Imperial Guard**   Plancenoit

NAPOLEON
72,000

Rossomme

Infantry
Cavalry
Artillery

1. 11.30 am Massed French guns open fire against Allied center. Reille's corps attacks Hougoumont. Large numbers of French troops bogged down throughout the day in fruitless struggle for possession.
2. 1.30 pm D'Erlon advances against Allied center. Massed ranks lose heavily from concentrated artillery fire, then engage Picton's division.
3. 2.00 pm Somerset and Ponsonby counterattack, routing most of D'Erlon's corps. Cavalry continues to attack the grand battery, but are nearly annihilated while attempting to return to friendly lines.
4. Diminutive King's German Legion garrison at La Haye Sainte defend their fortified position against an entire division, but manage to resist all attempts to break in.
5. About 3.30 pm Bülow's IV Corps approaches from Wavre. Believing Wellington is withdrawing, Ney launches massed cavalry attack. More and more cavalry committed without proper infantry or artillery support in futile attempt to break infantry squares.

on Picton's success. The Household Brigade under Lord Edward Somerset (1776–1842) and the Union Brigade under Sir William Ponsonby (1772–1815), stood to the west and east of the Brussels road, respectively.

The Heavy Brigade defeated opposing heavy cavalry moving in support of d'Erlon's left and struck the left flank and rear of the French division at the western end of the attacking column. The Union Brigade, on the other hand, had to advance through the friendly ranks of Picton's division, thus breaking up the cohesion of both formations. Still, by the time the cavalry descended the slope the French were in

retreat, and the cavalry consequently inflicted huge losses on them. 'The enemy's column,' wrote a British officer present in the charge, 'seemed very helpless, and had very little to fire on us from its front or flanks ... the front and flanks began to turn their backs inwards; the rear of the columns had already begun to run away.' Another officer noted that 'the enemy fled as a flock of sheep across the valley – quite at the mercy of the dragoons.' The charge, however, carried on with a momentum of its own and could not be stopped. The Scots Greys and others managed to penetrate all the way to the French guns, but were virtually destroyed by lancers in a stinging counterattack. Still, by 3.00 pm d'Erlon's attack had been first halted and then thrown back in disarray, while Wellington's line remained stable, if weakened.

The French made a second attempt to break the Allied line around 4.00 pm. In a reckless move, Ney, having provided no proper infantry or artillery support, launched 40 squadrons of cavalry – nearly 5,000 men – at the infantry deployed on the reverse slope of the ridge. The results were as Mercer described them: as the glittering horsemen approached, British batteries inflicted heavy losses before the crews ran for the protection of the infantry, which had formed squares for their own defense. The

Charge of the Scots Greys at Waterloo. In order to counter d'Erlon's massed infantry attack, the Earl of Uxbridge launched two brigades of cavalry, including this distinguished regiment. On catching the French completely by surprise, the Greys inflicted heavy casualties and took 2,000 prisoners and two Eagles. Overcome by their success, oblivious to danger and shouting 'Scotland Forever!', the troopers galloped on, sabering the gunners and drivers of a grand battery before being overwhelmed by French lancers and practically destroyed. (Ann Ronan Picture Library)

squares offered an effective fire of their own and the cavalry, however determined, could not break any of them. Ney repeated the attacks several times, each time with fewer men and at a slower pace. An unnamed British officer noted that the men grew increasingly confident once they saw off the cavalry in the first charge:

The first time a body of cuirassiers approached the square ... the men – all young soldiers – seemed to be alarmed. They fired high, and with little effect; and in one of the angles there was just as much hesitation as made me feel exceedingly uncomfortable; but it did not last long. No actual dash was made upon us ... Our men soon discovered that they had the best of it; and ever afterwards, when they heard the sound of cavalry approaching, appeared to consider the circumstance a pleasant change; for the enemy's guns suspended their fire.

By 5.30 pm the French cavalry, after suffering immense and futile losses, ceased the attack. British casualties were heavy nevertheless, for in the intervals between the cavalry charges the squares were especially vulnerable to French artillery fire. The location of many squares was marked by great piles of the dead lying in formation. Captain Gronow left a graphic description of the scene:

During the battle our squares presented a shocking sight. Inside we were nearly suffocated by the smoke and smell from burnt cartridges. It was impossible to move a yard without treading upon a wounded comrade, or upon the bodies of the dead; and the loud groans of the wounded and dying were most appalling.

At four o'clock our square was a perfect hospital, being full of dead, dying and mutilated soldiers. The charges of cavalry were in appearance very formidable, but in reality a great relief, as the artillery could no longer fire on us.

The fighting around La Haye Sainte was reaching its climax soon after the repulse of Ney's cavalry. As at Hougoumount, La Haye

Sainte had been under constant attack all day, and by late afternoon the infantry of the King's German Legion (KGL) inside had been drastically reduced in number, ammunition was nearly expended, and many of the buildings were ablaze. At 6.00 pm the French made a final thrust against the farm, where after desperate hand-to-hand fighting the attackers ejected the 40 survivors of an original garrison of 400. Two battalions of KGL infantry sent to the Germans' support from the ridge were destroyed by opposing cavalry, and French occupation of the place was confirmed. The fall of La Haye Sainte left Wellington's center very vulnerable, obliging him to concentrate every available infantry regiment and battery at this critical point. In addition he placed

Last stand of the Old Guard. As Napoleon's army was routed amid cries of 'Sauve qui peut!', three battalions of the Imperial Guard remained steadfast in square, vainly attempting to stem the Allied onslaught. Surrounded by overwhelming numbers of infantry and artillery, the Guard received concentrated fire at 60 yards, which wrought dreadful carnage. According to 19th century French historians, their commander, General Cambronne, refused the call to surrender with the heroic reply: 'The Guard dies but never surrenders', though eyewitnesses recorded the more prosaic response, 'Merde!' (Roger-Viollet)

two brigades of cavalry in the center rear. Despite the gallant defense shown throughout the day, the prospect of defeat now loomed large for the Allies.

Help was, however, now on its way. From 5.00 pm elements of the Prussian forces in action earlier in the day at Wavre had been arriving piecemeal from that village to the east and were engaging the French right in and around the village of Plancenoit. The Prussians were driven out by the Imperial Guard, but by 6.00 pm, when Wellington's line was at its most critical state, large numbers of Prussians were then arriving to retake Plancenoit and to oppose the French around La Haye and Papelotte, thus aiding Wellington's left as well as striking the French right further south. At last the Allies had managed to concentrate their forces and the French now faced a crisis of their own.

Napoleon believed he had a final opportunity to defeat Wellington before the Prussians could arrive and deploy in sufficient numbers to shift the balance unalterably against him. He ordered up seven battalions of the Imperial Guard from his reserve. These

Napoleon making plans on the eve of the battle. Blessed with an extraordinary ability to manage and maneuver large bodies of men on the march as well as on the battlefield, the Emperor generally formulated his plans alone before issuing orders to his various corps commanders. Yet even his most meticulous preparations could go awry when he found himself supplied with inferior troops, served by subordinates lacking his strategic and tactical genius, facing numerically superior forces, or a combination of all three. (Philip Haythornthwaite)

advanced up the slope between Hougoumont and the Ohain crossroads, intending to strike the Allied line, now considerably weakened from the day's fighting, and thus bring about its collapse. The French advanced slightly to the left toward two brigades, one under Sir George Cooke (1768–1837) and the other under Sir Colin Halkett (1774–1856). British guns fired on the advancing infantry but did not halt it; when the Imperial Guard reached the top of the ridge they were suddenly met by the Grenadier Guards, who rose from a prone position and unleashed a series of devastating volleys, causing the French to retire a short distance. The British Guards then charged, obliging the Imperial Guard to retire

Battle of Waterloo, 18 June 1815 (5.30 pm–8.00 pm)

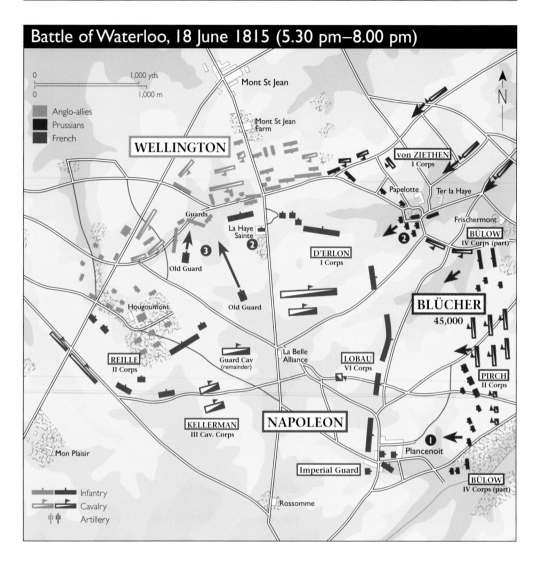

1. By 5.30 pm the Prussians are heavily engaged at Plancenoit, where Bülow is assisted by Pirch and Blücher himself. Prussians take the village, but are later ejected by Imperial Guard, Napoleon's last reserves.
2. Around 6.00 pm, Ney finally captures La Haye Sainte and brings up artillery to batter Allied center at close range. Wellington's line begins to waver. Perceiving this, Ney sends urgent appeals to Napoleon for attack by the Imperial Guard, but these are already engaged at Plancenoit. Zeithen's corps nears Wellington's left wing.
3. 7.00 pm The Old Guard, recalled from Plancenoit, attacks west of La Haye Sainte to confront Maitland's Guards Brigade and other formations. Fired on from three sides, the attackers recoil. At about the same time, approaching troops from the east recognized as Prussians, contributing to the French rout. Wellington orders a general advance and victory is assured.

again before reforming and returning up the slope. The same procedure was repeated, but on this occasion Napoleon's veterans were faced by a new threat, and failed to reform. From the right of the 1st Division had come a brigade under Major-General Adam (1781–1853) from the division of Sir Henry Clinton (1771–1829), containing the 52nd Foot, which deployed on the left flank of the Imperial Guard and fired enfilade into its wavering ranks. Confronted by deadly fire both to its front and flank, the Imperial Guard retreated, causing a general panic and rout of the entire French army. Wellington signaled a general advance of his entire line and the battle was won.

Europe restored and the Napoleonic legacy

The Vienna Settlement

Between November 1814 and June 1815 the leaders of Europe gathered in the Austrian capital for an international conference, later known as the Congress of Vienna, to fix the borders of European states in the aftermath of more than two decades of war. Although Napoleon had been overthrown and France defeated, the leaders of the victorious powers understood that neither the threat of war nor the future outbreak of revolution had been eradicated. The settlement which they sought at Vienna was, therefore, to a considerable degree intended to maintain peace and stability. Some leaders, like the arch counter-revolutionary Prince Metternich of Austria, wanted a league of sovereigns designed not only to preserve the settlement reached between them, but to enforce it as circumstances required anywhere on the Continent. This aim was theoretically possible, but in practice it would require at least basic cooperation between not only the victorious powers, but France as well.

To the leaders who gathered in Vienna, the French Revolution and the generation of war that arose out of it offered a stark lesson: radical political change, once begun, could not be controlled. Recent history had demonstrated that revolution brought with it political turmoil, civil war, regicide,

Sir Arthur Wellesley, First Duke of Wellington. Having risen to military greatness as C-in-C of Allied forces during the Peninsular War, his first and last encounter with Napoleon took place at Waterloo, where he deployed a mixed force of British, Hanoverians, Dutch, Belgians, Brunswickers, and Nassauers, most of whom were not the hardened veterans he had led to victory only a year before. Thus, without the timely intervention of Blücher's Prussians in the afternoon, history's most famous battle might well have ended inconclusively. (Philip Haythornthwaite)

military dictatorship, and years of war with the renegade power. If the French Revolution and Napoleon were indeed precedents of what Europe might face in the future, it was necessary for national leaders to take whatever steps were necessary to avoid future catastrophe.

Metternich firmly believed that rather than tame movements for economic, political or social reform as some advocated, it was better to smother the movement for change altogether before it gathered momentum. Stability was all-important to Metternich, who believed revolutions resulted from an international conspiracy of agitators. Austria, an empire of numerous nationalities, was particularly vulnerable to the nationalistic strain of revolution and the instability that war could bring. In effect, maintaining the

integrity of that empire became for him synonymous with the maintenance of peace on the Continent in general.

Metternich believed that two leading principles ought to be applied to the prevention of revolution and the problem of maintaining European peace and stability. According to the principle of legitimacy, nations should be monarchies with their rulers established on the basis of a strong claim, such as hereditary right. The relative effectiveness of a sovereign was secondary to his right to rule. Secondly, Metternich believed in the principle of intervention, which meant that in combating the spread of revolution across international borders, states that perceived a threat to themselves reserved the right to interfere in the internal affairs of other countries or to send troops to crush the movement, either unilaterally or in conjunction with other states.

The two men most responsible for the final reconstruction of the European states system were Metternich and Castlereagh. However, neither they nor the other politicians and sovereigns arrived at the Congress to begin with a clean slate. Many agreements between individual states already existed, some dating from 1813. Any product of their collective work would necessarily have to form a compromise of such deals and the conflicting views of the participants. Notwithstanding these complications, the various problems under discussion in Vienna could be settled by the application of three main principles.

First, rulers and states would be restored according to the principle of legitimacy. Metternich and Talleyrand were the main proponents of this principle, which provided dispossessed individual rulers or their dynastic successors with a restored throne on the basis of hereditary right. The powers gathered together in Vienna applied this principle to France, Spain, Piedmont, Tuscany, Modena, and the Papal States. After the First Treaty of Paris King Murat of Naples was permitted to retain his throne, though this was taken from him when, on Napoleon's return from Elba, he changed

sides during the Hundred Days, only to be defeated by the Austrians at Tolentino on 2–3 May and executed shortly thereafter.

The fact remained, however, that radically changed circumstances since 1792 rendered impossible the uniform application of this principle. This was particularly so in the case of Germany, where such fundamental political changes had taken place since the French Revolution that it was simply impossible to restore the more than 300 states that had previously existed. These were instead rationalized into 39 states and formed into the new German Confederation, administered by a diet at which each state was represented by a specified number of delegates. With her delegates acting as presidents of both chambers of the diet, Austria would exercise the leading influence. The principle of legitimacy could not be applied where it was deemed inconsistent with a particular state's security or self-interest.

The second principle applied at Vienna concerned territorial compensation. In short, the victorious states were to be rewarded at the expense of the defeated. The victorious powers not only expected to be rewarded for their contribution to Napoleon's defeat, but were determined that France and her allies should be penalized for their aggression. By the terms of the First Treaty of Paris, signed on 30 April 1814, France, largely at the behest of Castlereagh, was to face only moderate terms. France was to be restored to her frontiers of 1792; this still left her Savoy and the Saar, which between them provided an additional 500,000 inhabitants over her prewar population. Britain agreed to return all her captured French colonies except Mauritius, Tobago, and St Lucia. The victors imposed no indemnity on France and no army of occupation would remain on her soil. Nor would France have to return the thousands of pieces of looted art and treasures seized from Germany, Italy, Spain, and elsewhere over the past two decades. Britain retained the Cape of Good Hope from Holland in return for £2 million in compensation, but returned the valuable Dutch East Indies.

After the Hundred Days the Allies were far less forgiving, and the Second Treaty of Paris, signed on 20 November 1815, was much more punitive in nature. The French frontiers were reduced to those of 1790, the nation was to pay an indemnity of 700 million francs and an army of occupation would remain for three to five years to ensure that the indemnity was paid. But this is partly to anticipate the story, for the Congress had already concluded that France's allies were also to be punished, and it was largely at their expense that the four victorious Great Powers received territorial compensation.

Austria forswore all right to the Netherlands, which she had lost during the French Revolutionary Wars, but in exchange she received the northern Italian states of Lombardy and Venetia. To this was added the Tyrol from Bavaria and Illyria and Dalmatia on the eastern coast of the Adriatic.

Britain had no desire to acquire territory on the European continent. In satisfaction of her naval and maritime requirements she received Malta, the Ionian Islands in the Adriatic Sea, Heligoland in the North Sea, Cape Colony, and Ceylon.

Russia was to retain Finland, which she had seized from Sweden in 1808, together with the province of Bessarabia, which she had wrested from Turkey in the war of 1806–12. Sweden would in turn be compensated with Norway, itself taken from France's ally, Denmark. Most importantly, Russia received from Prussia most of her Polish provinces which she combined with her own to form a new Kingdom of Poland, with the Tsar at its head. It would not re-emerge as an independent state again until after the First World War.

Prussia, as noted above, gave up most of the territories she had taken from Poland during the partitions of 1772, 1793, and 1795. In exchange she received substantial compensation in the form of the Kingdom of Westphalia, Swedish Pomerania, most of the newly reconstituted Rhineland, and, above all, about 40 percent of the Kingdom of Saxony.

None of the Great Powers could be said to be completely contented with these arrangements, but by and large they were satisfied with the compromise.

Finally, the victorious Great Powers would make provision for the maintenance of peace in Europe. Two methods would be implemented to achieve this. First, France was to be ringed with buffer states forming a barrier between herself and her neighbors. To the north, as it was well recognized that Belgium could not defend herself unaided, she was amalgamated with Holland to produce a larger, more powerful state. In the south-east, Piedmont was augmented with Nice and Genoa in order to bolster the frontier with Italy. On France's eastern frontiers, Switzerland, known as the Swiss Confederation, was enlarged to 22 cantons, while the Rhineland became a Prussian possession.

Maintaining peace in Europe depended to a great extent on the balance of power. It was not sufficient to erect barriers to prevent France from committing future aggression without ensuring that the other Great Powers were themselves generally satisfied with the gains they themselves received. The fact remained that another state could threaten peace in the future, particularly Russia, who now possessed the greatest army in Europe. As Russia's acquisition of extensive Polish territory had greatly increased her power and influence, a balance was struck which granted Prussia much of Saxony. The Tsar had promised Prussia the whole of Saxony, but grave objections from Austria had nearly led to war and a compromise was finally agreed. The crisis had in fact reached such a point of contention that Britain, France, and Austria had secretly arranged an alliance should hostilities ensue with Prussia and Russia.

Assessing the Vienna Settlement

The relative success of the Vienna Settlement may be gauged by the fact that no general European war broke out for another 40 years, a

circumstance generally attributed to the fact
that it left no significant grievances
outstanding. However, it had its share of flaws.
The extensive territorial adjustments made at
Vienna took virtually no account of language,
culture or nationality. Any national aspirations
that the Belgians may have had had to be
subordinated to the perceived reality that their
tiny country could not stand alone against a
resurgent France. That the Belgians spoke
French and Flemish and were almost entirely
Catholic did not overly concern the men
tasked to redraw the map of Europe, who saw
amalgamation with a Protestant
Dutch-speaking Holland as the only option.
Much the same principle applied in northern
Italy, where French rule was for the most part
replaced with Austrian rule. On the other
hand, drastically reducing the number of
states in order to create the new German
Confederation paved the way for eventual
unification – for good or ill. The settlement
also stipulated that all the individual rulers
were to establish constitutions – an important
precedent on the path toward political
liberalization.

ABOVE The captive Napoleon on the deck of
HMS *Northumberland*, bound for St Helena. 'I desire to
live in England, a free man, protected by and subject to its
laws …', he had written in a bid for amnesty. With no desire
for a repetition of the escape from Elba, British authorities
refused and, accompanied by a suite of 15, Napoleon was
interned on one of the world's most inaccessible islands,
garrisoned by 3,000 British troops and patrolled by four
Royal Navy frigates. (Ann Ronan Picture Library)

RIGHT The Vienna Settlement graphically demonstrates
the extent to which the triumphant Great Powers
benefited territorially, and sought to create a buffer around
a possibly resurgent France, whose borders were restored
to those of prewar 1791. In general, frontiers shifted
westward: Russia kept Finland (taken from Sweden in
1809) and most Polish territory; Sweden received Norway
from France's ally Denmark; Prussia, in addition to a third
of Saxony, received substantial Rhenish territories that
greatly increased her presence in the north-west. Austria
made gains in northern Italy: two thirds of the Po Valley,
including the return of Milan and Mantua and the
annexation of Venice. Florence and Parma passed to minor
Habsburg rulers, thus rendering Austria the clearly
dominant power in Italy. Britain desired only off-shore
possessions: Heligoland in the North Sea and Malta and
the Ionian Islands in the Mediterranean. Belgium, too weak
to defend itself against France, was merged with Hollland
to create a more viable power. Similarly, the various
German states were loosely joined in a confederation to
ensure greater security.

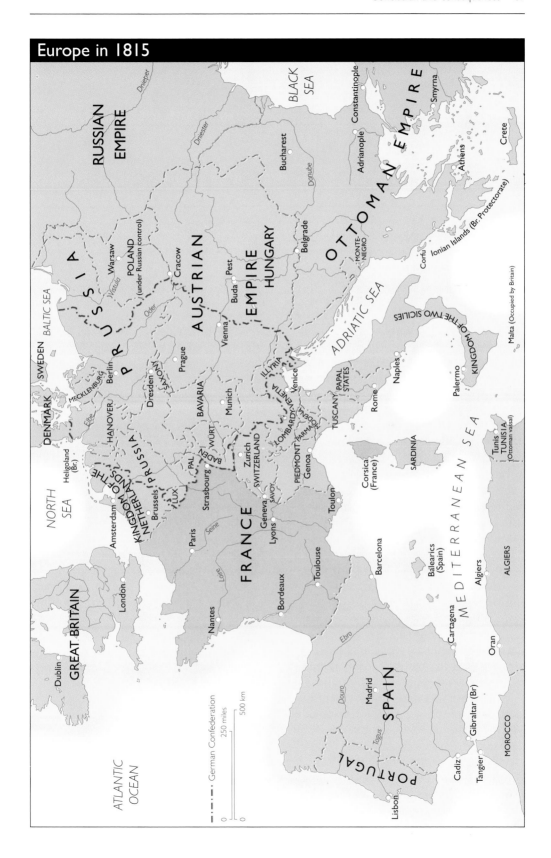

Europe in 1815

If the war had been won through the cooperation of the Great Powers it seemed reasonable to attempt to maintain peace and stability through some sort of 'concert' in the postwar era. Each power had differing ideas of how this could be accomplished, and in the case of Metternich, Great Power cooperation could also serve to combat revolution wherever it might arise. What has become known as the 'Congress System' was embodied in three documents: the Quadruple Alliance, Article VI of the Second Treaty of Paris of November 1815, and the Act of the Holy Alliance issued by Tsar Alexander in May of the same year.

Castlereagh in particular recognized that safeguarding the settlement required some sort of permanent arrangement, particularly with regard to the government of France. By the terms of the Quadruple Alliance, Russia, Austria, Prussia, and Britain agreed to cooperate for the next 20 years to prevent the accession of a Bonaparte dynasty to the throne of France. Article VI of the Treaty of Paris stipulated that future congresses would be convened in order for the Great Powers to discuss important issues of mutual concern and where necessary to take action in order to preserve European peace and stability.

A document with rather vaguely defined aims, the Holy Alliance, was drawn up by Alexander under the influence of Baroness von Krudener, a German religious mystic. This pseudo-religious document was intended to draw the sovereigns of Europe together on a personal and religious basis, whereby leaders and their peoples were to work together as one Christian body. Its wording was sufficiently

Longwood House, St Helena, the residence assigned to Napoleon. The approach was guarded by a company of infantry which established a ring of sentries at night. The governor of the island warned his sole captive that 'the orderly officer <u>must</u> see him daily, come what may, and may use any means he sees fit to surmount any obstacles or opposition … and that if the officer has not seen Napoleon by 10 o'clock in the morning he is to enter the hall and force his way to Napoleon's room.' (Philip Haythornthwaite)

obscure that practically every ruler agreed to it, apart from the Pope, the Sultan, and the Prince Regent. If it did not serve much practical use it was at least a basis for cooperation between Russia, Austria, and Prussia.

As a result of the Vienna agreement, four international conferences were held between 1815 and 1822 to discuss issues of mutual concern, particularly the outbreak of revolutions in Europe and the ongoing independence movements in South America. The period of congress diplomacy was short-lived, as it soon became apparent that the powers could not reach a consensus on a number of major issues, but the foundation of congress diplomacy at Vienna provided Europe with peace until the outbreak of the Crimean War in 1854 – even then a conflict with limited objectives and confined to Russia, France, Britain, and Turkey.

The Napoleonic legacy

Having abdicated a second time, Napoleon was sent a captive to the remote South Atlantic island of St Helena, from where he never again emerged to threaten European peace, and died there in 1821. Yet his influence scarcely ended with his death, for, despite only a decade in power, his legacy was far-reaching, both within France and throughout Europe as a whole.

It is important to consider what precisely accounted for Napoleon's extraordinary achievements. It is not to exaggerate the point to say that he was a genius, possessed of immensely wide knowledge and extraordinary powers of memory, for issues great and small. Natural intelligence accounted for his meteoric rise from a mere captain of artillery one year to brigadier-general the next, at the age of 23. He was a major-general at 26, he seized political power five years later and became Emperor at 35. By the time he was 40 he controlled most of the Continent. Apart from his unparalleled understanding of military affairs, he possessed considerable knowledge of civil administration, law, education, and science, to the point where many Napoleonic reforms remain in place today. Few historical figures, like Napoleon, leave their name and achievements to posterity, but he even has an era named for him.

He effected important religious reforms through his famous concordat with the Pope; sweeping civil and administrative reforms within France and throughout large parts of the empire reined in the excesses of the Revolution and gave order to inefficiency. Internally, France had well-functioning departments, newly re-opened primary schools and colleges of higher education. An antiquated legal system, based on French and German feudal principles, along with over 10,000 decrees issued under the Revolution, had been abolished, replaced in their turn by a new system – the *Code Napoléon*, or Civil Code. He went far in furthering the process of Italian and German unification, particularly in the latter's case, where he consolidated hundreds of petty principalities, free and ecclesiastical cities into a more rational entity – the Confederation of the Rhine.

Napoleon viewed himself as a consolidator rather than a promoter of the Revolution, and as early as December 1799, when he became First Consul, his government declared: 'Citizens, the Revolution is stabilized on the principles which began it.' His formulation of the Civil Code was an exceptional innovation, but apart from that he largely confined himself to preserving the reforms of the Revolution, which had ended so many of the laws and institutions of the *ancien régime*. Politically, he preserved a limited form of manhood suffrage and a constitution. Economically, he maintained the system that had abolished internal customs. In education, he established a national system. He preserved the revolutionary principle of equality before the law, the form of its administration and the principle of meritocracy – careers open to talent. Nevertheless, he did not, like the various revolutionary governments, permit much freedom to representative institutions; after all, the empire represented an autocracy.

Napoleon's remarkable military qualities enabled him to export the principles of the Revolution, and he styled himself a 'soldier of the Revolution'. Reforms made in France during the Revolution, Consulate and Empire were duly introduced, or sometimes imposed, in conquered territories, such as Holland, where Louis Bonaparte introduced the Napoleonic Code at his brother's behest. The Code became ensconced as far east as the Duchy of Warsaw, where the liberal-minded Alexander saw fit to allow retention of its central precepts, including equality before the law, even after the war. In some places, like in reactionary Spain, political and social reforms introduced in the wake of French armies had virtually no impact, notwithstanding the short-lived constitution established by Spanish liberals, but elsewhere, such as in Italy, Napoleonic reforms had a widespread and lasting – sometimes profound – impact.

As the Revolution had abolished serfdom in France, so too did Napoleon in many parts of Europe, particularly in western and southern Germany, and in Italy. Even in Naples, the poorest and politically most backward of Italian states, the restored King Ferdinand did not replace the Civil Code or re-establish the feudal system. Reactionaries generally succeeded in re-establishing some form of royal authority, but they simply could not reverse the myriad social and economic changes that had taken place during an absence from power which in some cases extended back a decade or more.

Napoleon's political legacy in Germany was particularly great, but the form it took in Prussia was not his work. It was a prime example of how a vanquished state endeavored to reform itself as a result of defeat – in this case a comprehensive one. As has been shown, in Prussia men like Yorck, Blücher, Scharnhorst, and Gneisenau utterly transformed not only the army, but society in general, to an extent that would lay the foundations of eventual German unification and the ascendancy of her army to the first rank on the Continent. The seeds of German nationalism were laid in the years 1807–15, and when wedded to militarism they would become a potent force that the French, invaded three times by Germany between 1870 and 1945, would bitterly regret.

Most of Napoleon's reforms were intended for the middle class, who benefited substantially from his regime. Legal rights were vastly extended, as were economic opportunities, and the stimulation to industry

specifically raised the standard of living for millions of French citizens. The natural by-product of this was, of course, a growth in political consciousness and a desire for further political concessions whose full manifestations would emerge during the revolution of 1830. The *bourgeoisie* in many occupied or conquered lands often saw Napoleon as a positive force for change, politically as well as economically. The Civil Code provided equality across class lines, administrative reforms abolished feudalism and ancient proprietary rights, and the aristocracy's powers, notwithstanding the technical victory of monarchy, dwindled as those of the middle classes rose. To be sure, improved legal rights outside France did not always bring immediate

The Congress of Vienna. After Napoleon's downfall the principal victors convened an international conference which met between November 1814 and June 1815. In addition to implementing the terms of the first Treaty of Paris and dismantling the Napoleonic Empire, the Congress's principal function was to re-draw the political map of Europe, restore the numerous dynasties to their respective thrones, provide territorial compensation to the victorious Great Powers, and to create a system for the preservation of peace and security on the Continent. (AKG, Berlin)

benefits to the peasants, and there was no remarkable improvement in their standard of living, but new principles of equality implanted some opportunities for social advancement and laid the groundwork for future economic developments.

In the field of arts and culture, it was natural that Napoleon should regard Paris – as indeed did so many Europeans – as the cultural center of Europe. He justified the looting of European art treasures on a massive scale in order to establish the ascendancy of the Louvre as the preeminent repository of paintings and sculpture. While his methods were extreme, the vast collection he assembled remains intact and continues to be appreciated by millions yearly. Napoleon had a particular interest in architecture, and the buildings he commissioned, inspired like so much else at the time by classical forms, generally assumed impressive proportions and continue to be admired today.

In the realm of military affairs, Napoleon's reputed quip on St Helena, while not entirely accurate, has much to be said for it: 'I have fought sixty battles, and I have learned nothing which I did not know in the beginning.' How then can we assess his military legacy? This question alone accounts for countless volumes on the subject, but a few brief observations may be offered here. Ironically, though he remained the central military figure for a generation, Napoleon did not emerge as a great military reformer, like Gustavus Adolphus or Frederick the Great, however much he may have inspired reforms in countries outside France. To the development of weapons and tactics he made some contributions, it is true, such as the use of massed artillery, but many of the changes that occurred had developed in the eighteenth century, particularly during the wars of the Revolution – such as the growth of mass armies.

Nevertheless, Napoleon rightly holds a place among the pantheon of great military commanders and it is important to understand both why this is so and why, notwithstanding this fact, he ultimately failed. First, Napoleon was extremely

industrious – a key element in a successful commander. Marshal Marmont noted that:

Whenever the moves of his headquarters allowed it, he went to bed at six or seven o'clock in the evening, and got up again at midnight or one o'clock. In this way he was ready to read reports as they came in and to give out his orders accordingly.

He was assiduous in keeping abreast of his enemies' movements and dispositions, and knowing the composition of his own forces. He placed great importance on accurate maps. During the 1813 campaign a Saxon officer serving as a topographical adviser on Napoleon's staff, noted that General Caulaincourt accompanied Napoleon everywhere with 'the necessary map fastened to his chest, because he always rode next to Napoleon so as to be able to hand it to him when he said, 'La carte ...' He was also a brilliant organizer, and it was a testament to Napoleon's genius and efficiency that he, supported of course by a nation nourished by past victories, was able to rebuild his armies twice in 1813 and again in 1814.

It must be stressed that he enjoyed the advantage of having inherited from the Revolution massive armies of men well motivated by the freedoms provided by merit. Capitalizing on this, Napoleon possessed the extraordinary ability to manage armies of hitherto unheard-of size – exceeding at times 200,000 men – and to move them across vast distances at rates never before conceived or achieved. Once his army reached the theater of campaign, Napoleon showed a masterful ability to maneuver this great mass of men, horses, and ordnance into a position from which he could exploit his enemies' generally consistent failure to concentrate their forces. In so doing, he could oppose and destroy forces in turn, or divide them if they had already combined. With respect to his own forces, he understood the vital importance of achieving – at the critical time – a local superiority of force and so wielding it to decisive advantage on such battlefields as Austerlitz and Jena. Even as late as the Waterloo campaign this strategy lay at the heart of his genius.

Wounded infantry on the field of Lützen, 2 May 1813. A group of fallen French soldiers hail their Emperor as he passes in the background. The grim side of Napoleonic warfare is unmistakably evident around them: the dead sprawled amidst the paraphernalia of war, including drums, muskets, equipment, and broken vehicles. Note the Russian grenadier (right), seated nonchalantly amongst his foes, taking some comfort from a flask doubtless containing rum or vodka. (Philip Haythornthwaite)

Yet where Napoleon failed to implement this strategy, or where his enemies denied him the opportunity to do so, he failed. Despite employing the largest army in history for the Russian campaign, Napoleon failed in part because he simply could not exercise the degree of personal control over his massive forces that was necessary for military success – much less to maintain political control over France. He failed to appreciate that the sheer size of his forces, combined with the primitive state of communications and agriculture in the area of operations, could not supply his vast needs, or enable him either to execute rapid marches or live off the land. Finally, the Russians, though they stood to oppose the French at Borodino, withdrew beyond the reach of the *Grande Armée*. To win, Napoleon needed to inflict a decisive blow on the opposing army. Alexander, however, denied him this satisfaction: he not only declined to fight, but went so far as to yield ground, including his capital, all territory that Napoleon could not ultimately retain. Through indecision and the mistaken belief that the Russians would come to terms, he postponed the retreat from Moscow until it was too late to avoid the

coming winter. In a greater geostrategic sense, he made the fatal mistakes later to be repeated by Hitler: leaving an undefeated enemy in his rear (Britain in the Peninsula) while trying to defeat a new opponent whose country was so vast and whose weather was so forbidding, as to swallow up even massive armies unprepared for winter conditions.

If Napoleon's personal form of leadership – his insistence on handling substantial bodies of troops largely on his own – often led to victory, it nevertheless served him ill where he could not be present to manage affairs. In planning and conducting a campaign largely by himself, he underlined his lack of confidence in his subordinates, the consequence of which was that he formulated no permanent staff system and therefore left no legacy on which to build one. This, instead, was taken up by the Prussians, who with their development of a permanent staff organization were ultimately to replace the French later in the century as the Continent's premier power.

In the end, excessive ambition and territorial overextension robbed Napoleon of permanent rule, both over Europe, as well as over France herself. Yet his legacy – the product of a mere decade in power – remains profound and enduring even today. Tens of thousands of books have been devoted to the Emperor's life and campaigns, and there is perhaps no greater testament to his enduring fascination than that this ever expanding body of literature continues to inspire and inform new generations of soldiers and civilians alike.

Further reading

Chalfont, Lord, ed., *Waterloo: Battle of Three Armies* (New York, Alfred Knopf, 1980).

Chandler, David, *The Campaigns of Napoleon* (London, Macmillan, 1966).

Dallas, Gregor, *The Final Act: The Roads to Waterloo* (New York, Henry Holt, 1996).

Delderfield, R. F., *Imperial Sunset: The Fall of Napoleon, 1813–14* (New York, Stein and Day, 1980).

Elting, J. R., *Swords Around a Throne: Napoleon's Grande Armée* (London, Weidenfeld & Nicolson, 1988).

Esposito, V. and Elting, J. R., *A Military History and Atlas of the Napoleonic Wars* (New York, Praeger, 1964, repr. London, Greenhill Books, 1999).

Hamilton-Williams, David, *The Fall of Napoleon: The Final Betrayal*, (London, Arms and Armour Press, 1994).

Haythornthwaite, Philip, *The Napoleonic Sourcebook* (London, Arms and Armour Press, 1990).

Henderson, E. F., *Blucher and the Uprising against Napoleon* (New York, G. P. Putnam's Sons, 1911).

Hofschröer, Peter, *Leipzig 1813* (Oxford, Osprey Publishing, 1993, repr. 2000).

— *Lützen and Bautzen 1813* (Oxford, Osprey Publishing, 2001).

Howarth, David, *Waterloo: Day of Battle* (New York, Athaneum, 1968).

Lawford, James, *Napoleon: The Last Campaigns, 1813–15* (New York, Crown Publishers, 1977).

Mercer, Cavalié, *Journal of the Waterloo Campaign* (London, Blackwood, 1870, repr. New York, Da Capo Press, 1995).

Murray, Venetia, *High Society in the Regency Period, 1788–1830* (London, Penguin, 1998).

Nafziger, George, *Lützen and Bautzen: Napoleon's Spring Campaign of 1813* (Chicago, 1992).

— *Napoleon at Dresden: The Battles of August 1813* (Rosemont, IL, Emperor's Headquarters, 1991).

— *Napoleon at Leipzig: The Battle of the Nations 1813* (Rosemont, IL, Emperor's Headquarters, 1997).

Nicholson, Harold, *The Congress of Vienna: A Study in Allied Unity, 1812–1822* (London, Constable, 1948, repr. New York, Harvest Books, 1974).

Palmer, Alan, *Metternich* (New York, Harper & Row, 1972).

Paret, Peter, *Yorck and the Era of Prussian Reform* (Princeton, Princeton University Press, 1966).

Petre, F. Loraine, *Napoleon at Bay, 1814* (London, John Lane, 1914, repr. London, Arms & Armour Press, 1977).

— *Napoleon's Last Campaign in Germany, 1813* (London, John Lane, 1912, repr. London, Arms & Armour Press, 1977).

Shanahan, W. O., *Prussian Military Reforms, 1786–1813* (New York, Columbia University Press, 1945).

Smith, Digby, *1813 Leipzig: Napoleon and the Battle of the Nations* (London, Greenhill Publishing, 2001).

Webster, Sir Charles, *The Congress of Vienna, 1814–1815* (New York, Barnes & Noble, 1963).

Webster, Sir Charles, *The Foreign Policy of Castlereagh, 1812–1815: Britain and the Reconstruction of Europe* (London, G. Bell and Sons, 1931).

Wooten, Geoffrey, *Waterloo 1815* (Oxford, Osprey Publishing, 1999).

Index

Related titles & companion series from Osprey

CAMPAIGN (CAM)

**Strategies, tactics and battle experiences
of opposing armies**

WARRIOR (WAR)

**Motivation, training, combat experiences
and equipment of individual soldiers**

ELITE (ELI)

**Uniforms, equipment, tactics and personalities
of troops and commanders**

NEW VANGUARD (NVG)

**Design, development and operation
of the machinery of war**

ORDER OF BATTLE (OOB)

**Unit-by-unit troop movements and
command strategies of major battles**

Contact us for more details – see below

ESSENTIAL HISTORIES (ESS)

**Concise overviews of major wars
and theatres of war**

MEN-AT-ARMS (MAA)

**Uniforms, equipment, history
and organisation of troops**

To order any of these titles, or for more information on Osprey Publishing, contact:

Osprey Direct (UK)   *Tel:* +44 (0)1933 443863   *Fax:* +44 (0)1933 443849   *E-mail:* info@ospreydirect.co.uk

Osprey Direct (USA) c/o MBI Publishing   *Toll-free:* 1 800 826 6600   *Phone:* 1 715 294 3345

Fax: 1 715 294 4448   *E-mail:* info@ospreydirectusa.com

www.ospreypublishing.com

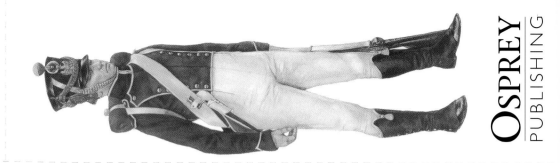

OSPREY PUBLISHING

FIND OUT MORE ABOUT OSPREY

❑ Please send me a FREE trial issue of Osprey Military Journal

❑ Please send me the latest listing of Osprey's publications

❑ I would like to subscribe to Osprey's e-mail newsletter

Title/rank _____

Name _____

Address _____

_____

_____

_____

Postcode/zip _____

State/country _____

E-mail _____

Which book did this card come from?

_____

❑ I am interested in military history

My preferred period of military history is _____

❑ I am interested in military aviation

My preferred period of military aviation is _____

I am interested in (please tick all that apply)

❑ general history   ❑ militaria   ❑ model making

❑ wargaming   ❑ re-enactment

Please send to:

USA & Canada:
Osprey Direct USA, c/o MBI Publishing,
PO Box 1, 729 Prospect Ave, Osceola, WI 54020, USA

UK, Europe and rest of world:
Osprey Direct UK, PO Box 140, Wellingborough,
Northants, NN8 2FA, United Kingdom

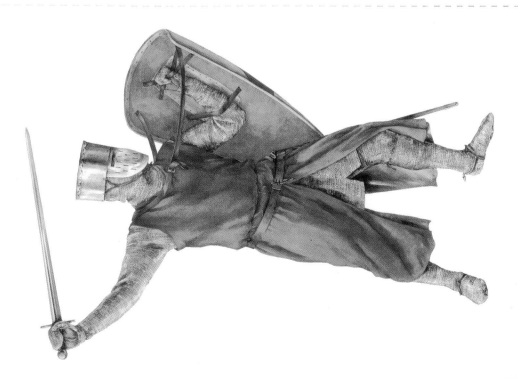

OSPREY
PUBLISHING

www.ospreypublishing.com

call our telephone hotline
for a free information pack

USA & Canada: 1-800-826-6600
UK, Europe and rest of world call:
+44 (0) 1933 443 863

Young Guardsman
Figure taken from *Warrior 22:*
Imperial Guardsman 1799–1815
Published by Osprey
Illustrated by Christa Hook

POSTCARD

Knight, c.1190
Figure taken from *Warrior 1: Norman Knight 950 – 1204AD*
Published by Osprey
Illustrated by Christa Hook

www.ospreypublishing.com